THE GLORY DAYS:

From the Life of Luther Allan Weigle

COMPILED BY RICHARD D. WEIGLE

Richard D. Weigle

FRIENDSHIP PRESS • NEW YORK

Library of Congress Cataloging in Publication Data

Weigle, Luther Allan, 1880-
The glory days: from the life of Luther Allan Weigle.

Bibliography: p.
1. Weigle, Luther Allan, 1880- 2. Congregational churches–Sermons.
3. Sermons, American. 4. Weigle, Luther Allan, 1880- –Bibliography.
I. Title.
BX7260.W444A33 285'.8' 0924 [B] 76-21779
ISBN 0-377-00058-2

contents

foreward

As my father advanced through his eighties, he conceived the thought of publishing what he termed his memorabilia. This was not to be an autobiography in the generally understood meaning of the word. But it would be autobiographical in that he proposed to bring together certain articles and sermons from different periods of his life, writings which he thought would present his concerns as a Christian educator, scholar and administrator, and which would provide a chronological guide to the development of his thinking. We, four of his children, all encouraged him in his endeavor, both out of familial pride in our father's life and out of the conviction that such a book would prove both interesting and stimulating to the wide constituency of his colleagues, his associates and his friends.

The project moved slowly. Not until he had relinquished the chairmanship of the Standard Bible Committee upon his ninetieth birthday did he seriously begin work on the memorabilia. A series of prospective tables of content, both typed and written in his characteristic handwriting, bear witness to his efforts to select the most appropriate writings for the proposed volume. One such draft bears the simple title, "My Faith and Work." His able and devoted secretary, Mrs. Anne Temple, worked with him, preparing the material as he determined it. Several times he suggested to me that he simply abandon the project. On these occasions I would urge him to proceed at whatever pace his strength would permit. As time went on, the effort proved too great, and the project lapsed. I assured him that the book was merely postponed and that I would assume responsibility for its publication once we had resolved the matter of the contents.

The initial chapter entitled "The Religious Education of a Protestant" was always my father's choice to begin the memorabilia. It describes his own religious education in a minister's family, at a Lutheran college and seminary, and at a great university. Subsequent chapters 3 and 4 deal with his thirty-four years of service at Yale Divinity School and with the four major chairmanships which marked his great contributions to the church and to the cause of Christian unity. These appointments were all of long duration: twenty years chairing the executive committee of the American Association of Theological Schools, thirty years chairing the executive committee of the World's Sunday School Association, nine years chairing the planning committee for the National Council of Churches in the United States of America, and thirty-six years chairing the Standard Bible Committee, the committee of scholars that produced the Revised Standard Version of the Bible. My father never wrote his own accounts of two of these chairmanships, those dealing with the theological schools and the National Council. For these two sections we are indebted to Dr. Gerald E. Knoff, one of my father's former students who was closely associated with him over the years, especially when Dr. Knoff served as Associate General Secretary for Christian Education of the National Council of Churches.

Chapter 10 is a reprinting of my father's Introduction to the 1966 edition of Horace Bushnell's *Christian Nurture*. This work had contributed profoundly to my father's thinking. He once wrote that, with the possible exception of some of Jonathan Edwards' writings, "no American book can with better right be deemed a religious and educational classic." Four of my father's sermons were selected by him to be included and now compose chapters 6, 7, 8 and 9.

Concluding the book is a comprehensive bibliography of his writings, most of which are now deposited in the Sterling Memorial Library at Yale University.

As an appendix to the volume, there are two short pieces written by my sister, Ruth Weigle Guyton. Both are quite personal in nature. Both were addressed to my father. The first was written as a tribute to our mother, Clara Boxrud Weigle, a year after her death in 1965. The second my sister wrote as a love letter to our father on Valentine's Day during his ninety-fifth year. What my sister has written reveals in beautiful and moving fashion the great human and personal sides of both our father and our mother. The two pieces demonstrate that, just as my father wrote of the influence his parents and his home had upon him, so he and our devoted mother profoundly shaped the way in which their children were to live. A quotation from the final paragraph of the letter furnishes the title for this volume. My sister wrote: "Those were the glory days." And indeed they were.

The reader is reminded that the material comprising the several chapters of this volume covers a productive lifetime. A conscious decision was reached not to alter what had been written to make it conform to later thinking or experience. For example, no quotations from the Revised Standard Version of the Bible appear in any of the writings or sermons which date back to the period before 1946.

To all those who have graciously given permission to republish articles or sermons which previously appeared in books, journals and other publications I should like to express my appreciation. I am most grateful that my father's dream of collecting his writings has now become a published reality. In these expressions of thanks I am joined by my father, by my brother, Dr. Lüther Allan Weigle, Jr., and by my two sisters, Margaret Weigle Quillian and Ruth Weigle Guyton.

In concluding this foreword, let me quote the final two paragraphs from the first chapter of the book. They seem to epitomize the goals, the philosophy and the faith of a great Christian.

Protestantism finds its most definite assurance of the divine fatherhood in the life and teaching, the death and resurrection, of him who most completely fulfilled his sonship to God–Jesus Christ. It is not merely as an ethical teacher or even as an example of what human life may be that Jesus Christ is the central figure in human history. It is because He is more than an historical figure. It is because He affords us a glimpse of ultimate Reality, because we see in Him the character and disposition of God dwelling among us, because God was in Christ reconciling the world unto Himself. That vision of God in Christ is the gospel of Protestantism; its evidence is the power that it has exerted throughout the centuries, and that it now has, to awaken conscience, to inspire love and trust, and to save us from folly and wrong. When we affirm belief in the living, eternal Christ, we declare our conviction that the character and disposition of God thus glimpsed is consistently true and forever dependable.

Protestantism is not an organization. It is a spirit; a way of thinking and living. To realize this gospel in my own life, and to equip young people to be its effective ministers, is my vocation.

Richard D. Weigle

St. John's College
Annapolis, Maryland

1

THE RELIGIOUS EDUCATION OF A PROTESTANT

When, at the age of thirty-five, I resigned the John Chandler Williams Professorship of Philosophy in Carleton College to accept appointment to the newly established Horace Bushnell Professorship of Christian Nurture in the Divinity School of Yale University, I made it my first business to read Bushnell's book on *Christian Nurture*, with which I had been acquainted only at second hand, principally through the references made to it by Professor George A. Coe. I confess that I took it up with some misgiving, wondering whether or not it contained old ideas and outworn forms of thought that might tend to limit the freedom of the incumbent of the new chair.

I found just the opposite. Old though the book was, the vitality and vigor of Bushnell's thought proved to be emancipating. I read and reread *Christian Nurture* and subsequently edited it for appearance in a new edition, with interest and enthusiasm. And I wrote a long letter to my father about it, with all the zest of one who has made a discovery, outlining to him its main positions and telling him of my happiness to find so free a charter for the new work that I was undertaking.

My father replied that he agreed with all that I had written about Bushnell's book, which he had known and prized ever since his own days as a theological student. In proof of this, he sent me his copy, bought and first read in 1876, bearing evidences of much use and with margins well marked and annotated at most of the points that I had so eagerly commended to him. Then I made a real discovery—that Bushnell was but describing what I had seen and known and shared through-

This autobiographical account was first published in *Contemporary American Theology: Theological Autobiographies*, edited by Vergilius Ferm. New York: Round Table Press, Inc., 1932.

out the whole of my life, that the spirit of my father and mother was akin to his, and that I was myself a child of Christian nurture.

My father was a minister, and my mother–I now know–an ideal minister's wife. My early education in religion was through the influence and associations, the habits and conditionings of life in the home of a Christian minister who sincerely believed in his work and thoroughly enjoyed it. Religion was a naturally accepted baseline for all of our life and thought. There was nothing strained or morbid or professional about it. My childhood was thoroughly happy and normal –at least it seemed so then, whenever I stopped to think about it, which I very seldom did; and it seems so now, as I look back upon it.

As a family, we shared in a number of religious observances. We gave thanks to God as we gathered for our meals; we engaged in a brief service of family worship after breakfast each morning; we read the Bible and books of Bible stories and memorized great passages of Scripture that father selected for us; we studied Luther's *Small Catechism* and the Sunday school lessons; we went together to public worship in the church, to prayer meetings and Sunday school, to missionary societies and the Band of Hope. Some of these observances were required of us children, and some were not; but none of them bore down upon us with the weight of compulsion. They so obviously meant a great deal to father and mother that we were glad to share in them. We had ample time and freedom for other things also–for reading and work and play. And I now see that deeper than any or all of these observances was the spirit of love and good fellowship that so constantly lighted our life together–a spirit that likewise was accepted by us as a matter of course. If we thought about it at all, which I cannot remember that we did, I am sure that we had difficulty distinguishing between the love of God and the love of father and mother–a predicament that is not undesirable for youngsters and that does not worry them in the least.

The church that my father served for the nine years that carried me from the age of six to that of fifteen had a large membership–and fostered a wide range of activities from oyster suppers and dramatic entertainment to cottage prayer meetings and revivals. I attended most of these. There were no motion pictures in those days, dancing and cards were frowned on, and my parents were rightfully dubious about the few shows and plays that came to our local theater; so in all honesty, it must be admitted that the church was one of my best available sources of entertainment.

It was a Lutheran church, belonging to the least conservative of the Lutheran bodies, the General Synod; and it was different from most

Lutheran churches in an evangelistic temper that inclined it toward "new measures," revivals, and "protracted meetings." My father would not employ an itinerant revivalist; he believed that each minister should be an evangelist in his own pulpit and to his own people. Among my most vivid memories stand out the protracted meetings that I attended in the large lecture room of the church, when for six to eight weeks between the first of January and Easter, my father would preach on every weeknight except Saturday, as well as twice on Sunday, extending to sinners the invitation of the gospel and calling upon them to repent and be converted. Folk did repent and were converted under his preaching; each year, after a suitable period of instruction, many such were received into the membership of the church. One year, as people began to stand and ask for the prayers of the church and to come forward to the seats that had taken the place of the older "mourners' bench," I wanted to join them. When I told my father of my desire, he replied that I need not wait until the invitation would be given in the public meeting that evening, but that I could come to God at once, in the privacy of his study, and that he would be glad right then to talk with me about any of my questions or problems, and to pray with me. I accepted his invitation; and he turned what was a first, I fear, mere suggestibility into a genuine religious experience.

My father was an effective teacher. In accordance with the time-honored custom of the Lutheran churches, he conducted classes in preparation for church membership, one of which, for children ten to fourteen years of age, met on Saturday afternoons from October to Easter, and the other, for young people and adults, met on Friday evenings for the same term. The work of these classes was based on Luther's *Small Catechism*, but it was far from the meager, formal memorization that many associate with the idea of catechization. In a simple, vivid, interesting way, it covered the main points of Christian belief and practice. I had four years of this work, two in each class. In my last year, when I was a sophomore in high school, I outlined its content; and I was surprised to find when I reached the theological seminary six years later that this was a fairly good outline of the elementary principles of systematic theology. If any reader is disposed to comment that this only proves that my father taught theology to his people, I answer that in my judgment that is what every minister ought to do, that classes such as my father conducted would benefit every church, and that the systematic theology taught in our seminaries ought to be vital enough in content to be adaptable to such use.

In another class for young people and adults, meeting on Wednesday evenings after the weekly prayer meeting, my father conducted systematic Bible study of the sort made popular by Dwight L. Moody in the 1880s. I joined this class also and greatly enjoyed it. I learned more from these classes taught by my father than from all my years as a pupil in the Sunday school.

My mother recently gave me a scrapbook in which she had treasured newspaper clippings of family interest. In it, I found a group of reports of sermons preached by my father forty years ago, with a short clipping that acknowledges my services as reporter. The latter recalls "the thrill that comes once in a lifetime." Here it is, under the date of July 4, 1882: "For the report of a number of sermons recently preached by Rev. Mr. Weigle, of the First Lutheran Church, THE TIMES is under obligation to that gentleman's little son, Luther Weigle, who, although but 11 years of age, handles the pen with a vigor and discrimination which would be creditable to one of more mature years."

I have quoted that because it indicates how intimately my father let me be associated with his work. I was always free to browse in his library and, of course, to go to him for counsel and source materials when I had to write an essay or prepare for a debate. Better yet, as I became able to do it, he let me begin to work with him. He bought me a typewriter, and I often typed for him the manuscript or outline of one of his sermons for the coming Sunday. Here again, there was no compulsion; he did not exploit me, and I am sure that he could have preached quite as well from his own notes as from my typescript. But I liked the work, and it became a sort of informal apprenticeship in theology and homiletics that contributed to my education.

Let no one think that this was undue domination of my mind. It was simply that my father shared with me, in the measure of my boyish capacity, his interests, his convictions, and his work. There was remarkable freedom in our relations. He let me enter with him into the realm where reality and truth lay for him, then encouraged me to do my own thinking and to make my own decisions. What better thing could a parent do? It is a decadent generation that cherishes no beliefs and holds no convictions that it cares to transmit to its children and fondly imagines that they will achieve freedom if they are let alone to discover everything for themselves and to do as they please, without information, guidance, or discipline.

Two of my father's sayings, in this connection, have stayed in my memory and grow more meaningful as the years pass and my own sons and daughters are growing into manhood and womanhood. One of these sayings dates back to my early childhood. When I would say, as children will, "Daddy, when I grow up, I want to be just like you," he would laughingly answer, "Then I'll be ashamed of you because you must stand on my shoulders." The other was but a few years before his death, in 1923. In the course of social conversation, my father and I expressed differing judgments on some point, whether of politics or theology, and a member of the group who possessed more initiative than tact called attention to this divergence of view—"Why, Dr. Weigle, your son does not believe as you do." He answered, "My son believes as I think I would believe if I faced his problems and had his work."

Horace Bushnell had a great phrase to describe the goal of parental instruction and discipline—"the emancipation of the child." My father's dealing with me was in the spirit of that phrase. Evidence of this is afforded by the fact that ultimately I made important decisions that were not in line with his own desires—I chose college teaching as my vocation rather than the preaching ministry; my work took me away from the Lutheran into the fellowship of the Congregational churches; and finally, I felt obliged to decline a position that had always been his dearest ambition for me. Yet we had no word of dissension over these decisions, and he never made me feel that my choice of another path was an act of disloyalty to him.

One decision I made as a freshman in college was an act of disloyalty. I became a member, secretly, of an organization that my father had forbidden me to join, in spite of the fact that he was providing for the full expense of my education and that even the dues that I paid to this organization were a part of his bounty. For four years throughout my college course and for one year more in theological seminary, I kept up this deception. Then came an evening in the summer vacation when, as I was preaching to an audience of young people in a distant town, I sharply realized my unworthiness to preach to others while my own life cherished this lie. I wrote a long letter to my father, confessed what I had done, told him how sorry I was, asked his forgiveness, and promised to repay what I had so spent. In answer, I received a telegram: "It is all right. I forgive you. I knew it two days after you did it." Then I could look back and could see how on various occasions throughout those five years he had made some approach that afforded me the chance to tell him what he already knew. Although I failed him, he waited and loved me anyhow. He did not fail me, did not give me up.

I count that one of my life's crucial experiences. Shame for my misdeed and relief at my father's forgiveness gave way to a flash of illumination and was transcended in the wonder and joy of a new insight. That insight was not only into unsuspected depths of my father's character; it was a new vision of the fatherhood of God. My father's love and patience and understanding became to me a revelation of the love and patience and understanding of God. I had found the gospel. I had a message to preach, a faith to live by. What I had before heard and learned about God, I now saw for myself and understood. I could say with Job: "I had heard of Thee by the hearing of the ear; but now mine eye seeth Thee."

Some years later, I read Royce's discussion of atonement, in *The Problem of Christianity*. Atonement takes place, he says, when an act of wrong becomes the occasion for another act of such creative, redemptive quality that the final result is better than it would have been if the wrong act had not been done. In just that sense, my father made atonement for the wrong that I had done to him. His deed was such that all was better in the end. My deception was not blurred over or blotted out; it remained wrong. But he met it with a love so resourceful as to transmute its consequences to good.

I came to see that God does likewise with human sin. He makes even the wrath of men to praise Him, not because He crushes it with power, but because He overcomes it with love. That is the meaning of the divine atonement in Jesus Christ. I saw why Martin Luther so prized John 3:16, the verse that he said contains the gospel in miniature: "God so loved the world, that he gave his only begotten Son, that whosoever believeth on him should not perish, but have eternal life." I was helped, too, by the writings of two men who were not of Lutheran but of Calvinistic heritage. President Charles Cuthbert Hall's little book on *The Gospel of the Divine Sacrifice* came into my hands, as it happened, within a day or two after I had received my father's message, and it gave me an illuminating statement of principle: "The atonement not the cause of God's love, but God's love the cause of the atonement." I was profoundly stirred by Professor A. B. Bruce's definition of the Kingdom of God: "The reign of divine love exercised by God in His grace over human hearts believing in His love and constrained thereby to yield Him grateful affection and devoted service."

In one of the essays in *The Will to Believe*, William James pictures the relation of man to God in a striking figure. Man may be like a novice at chess playing against an expert. The novice is eager and confident; he may by chance make some good moves; he will surely make poor ones. The expert does not know what moves the novice will make, but he does not need to know. He understands how to meet every possible move, and the issue of the game is certain. The expert will win.

This is an exceedingly suggestive analogy. But it is in one respect misleading. In the chess game, one player must lose. If the expert wins, the novice loses; if the novice wins, the expert loses. It is not so in the game of life. God is not our opponent; He is no enemy to be outplayed or outwitted. Life is a game where both players win or both lose. If we win, God wins; if we lose, He suffers defeat. We must play with Him, not against Him.

James's analogy would be closer to the truth if it were stated in terms of the pupil-teacher relation, or the relation of son to father. The teacher does not know what mistakes his pupil will make, but he knows how to meet and correct them. The father does not know what ambitions his son will conceive, what good sense or what folly will possess him; but if he be as wise as fathers ought to be, he will meet whatever happens in such ways as to further the son's development into free, right-minded, and responsible manhood. Here is not opposition, but community of interest. If the pupil wins, the teacher wins; if the pupil fails, the teacher loses. If the son wins, the father wins; if the son is defeated in the game of life, the father is defeated too. So it is with God, if God is what Jesus revealed Him to be—our Father.

At Gettysburg College, I was most stimulated by the work in logic, by a rigorous course in Noah Porter's *Elements of Intellectual Science*, and by four years' study of Greek under Professor Oscar G. Klinger. After three years of training in Greek in the secondary school, I was prepared to enjoy Greek literature and found in Klinger a most interesting teacher. Best of all, he introduced me to Greek philosophy. We did not get into it very deeply, but his lectures and my reading of a textbook in the history of Greek philosophy gave me an elementary knowledge of its main currents; we translated several of Plato's dialogues and browsed about in Burnet's *Early Greek Philosophers*. An incidental result was that I became absorbingly interested in the writings of Walter Pater, especially his *Plato and Platonism*, *Marius the Epicurean*, and the *Essay on Style*.

The only course in biology that I took in college was one on human physiology, but I was brought into contact with the theory of evolution by the work in geology. Again aided and abetted by Professor Klinger, I did a good deal of reading on this subject in my senior year, being especially concerned with its implications for ethics and theism. Among the first books, outside of textbooks, that I bought for my personal library were some that I read then—Spencer's *First Principles*; Thomas H. Huxley's *Evolution and Ethics*; John Fiske's *Destiny of Man*, *Idea of God*, and *Through Nature to God*. I spent most of the summer vacation following graduation from college in writing out my reaction to these volumes, under the modest title, "Some Notes on the Genesis of Sin." I submitted it for publication to *The Independent*, but it never appeared in print, and when, after the lapse of some months, I wrote to inquire, the editor answered that he had seen no such manuscript. So perished my first serious literary effort. I knew by that time, however, that it was no loss to the world, for I had been doing more reading and had found more light in Henry Drummond's *The Ascent of Man*, George Harris's *Moral Evolution*, and

E. Griffith-Jones's *The Ascent Through Christ.* I entered the theological seminary with my ideas fairly well straightened out on that issue; I was convinced that one could accept the scientific principle of evolution and yet hold to the Christian conception of God and the Christian view of human life.

For two years, I was a student in the Lutheran Theological Seminary at Gettysburg, where I was most helped by President Valentine in systematic theology and Dr. Edmund J. Wolf in New Testament and church history. We got practically nothing of the modern critical method as applied to the Old Testament; Dr. Wolf, although generally conservative in his conclusions, gave us a fair idea of the methods of historical and literary criticism as applied to the New Testament. As for many beginners in theological study, my central problem was that of the value of the Biblical studies. It did not shape itself, however, as it does for some today, into a doubt of the value of history in general; the most radical of us in the first years of the twentieth century were too conservative to think of that. My question was rather about the meaning and method of revelation and inspiration. In what sense is the Bible the Word of God? My teachers at the Seminary afforded excellent guidance at this point, for they took the Christocentric view of the Scriptures that was characteristic of Luther, disavowed mechanical theories of inspiration, and taught that the divine revelation is progressive, not because God holds back truth, but because it is relative to occasions and suited to the capacity of man the recipient. I was greatly helped by a little book by President William DeWitt Hyde, entitled *God's Education of Man.* As a student at Yale, I read Bruce's *The Chief End of Revelation* and Ladd's massive *Doctrine of Sacred Scripture*, with the result that when William Newton Clarke's *Sixty Years with the Bible* appeared some dozen years later I found that it had no particular message for me–I had long since made the adjustments he described, or had never needed to make them.

The study of the Bible has always interested me, and much of my reading is in Biblical history and theology. For several years, I taught a course to seniors at Carleton on the philosophy of the Christian religion, for which we used as common reading the admirable volume by Professor A. B. Bruce entitled *Apologetics, or Christianity Defensively Stated.* It is now forty years old, and its philosophical section is out-of-date, but its sections dealing with Biblical history and literature seem to me to be yet worth reading.

In the second year at the Seminary, my interest centered about the problems of the person and work of Jesus Christ. I read a great deal, and in more substantial books. Among those that helped me most were two that are now almost, if not quite, forgotten, D. W. Simon's *Recon-*

ciliation by Incarnation and Thomas Adamson's *Studies of the Mind in Christ*; and two that were widely influential, Principal Fairbairn's *The Place of Christ in Modern Theology* and D. W. Forrest's *The Christ of History and of Experience.* It is a subject that has never been far from my thought, and to list the books that have contributed to my thinking upon it throughout the years would make this work unduly bibliographical. I mention just a few of the most stimulating –Adolf Harnack's *What Is Christianity?*, Forrest's *The Authority of Christ*, Mackintosh's *The Doctrine of the Person of Jesus Christ*, Rashdall's *The Idea of Atonement in Christian Theology*; and I cannot forbear a word of greatful acknowledgment of the recent book by Professor John Baillie on *The Place of Jesus Christ in Modern Christianity*, the trenchant study of *The Mind of Christ in Paul* by my colleague, Professor Frank C. Porter, and Canon Raven's *Jesus and the Gospel of Love*.

For a period of several months during my first year at the Seminary, Professor Klinger was ill, and the authorities of the college asked me to teach some of his classes in Greek. I lay awake most of the night before meeting my first class. I had never taught, and these students had been sophomores when I was a senior. I had visions of their trying me out by some of the ways of annoying a teacher that I knew so well. But they treated me fairly, and I so enjoyed the experience of teaching that I began to think that it might be my vocation. In the following year, I gave half-time to teaching in the academy associated with the college, and then my mind was made up. I wanted to teach and must go on for graduate study. Should it be in Greek? I debated that, but finally decided for philosophy and for Yale. My decision had been helped by counseling with Professor Klinger, who wanted me to study with Professor George T. Ladd and gave me eight volumes of Ladd's works as a parting gift.

The decision to prepare for teaching did not involve forsaking my ambition to become a Lutheran minister. College teaching was a well-recognized form of ministerial service, and many members of college faculties preached more or less regularly. I supplied Messiah Church, Harrisburg, during the summer before entering the Yale Graduate School, and was licensed to preach by the East Pennsylvania Synod. In the summer of 1903, after a year at Yale, I served as missionary pastor of the newly organized church at Mount Union, Pennsylvania; and in September, having been called to the pastorate of the First Lutheran Church of Bridgeport, Connecticut, I presented myself for ordination at the meeting of the Allegheny Synod. One of my former teachers at Gettysburg objected strenuously. He based his objection not on any lack of preparation or any defect in doctrine, although he felt that my views were a bit too synergistic, and he had heard me deliver a sermon in which I used an illustration drawn from William James's classic chapter on "Habit," which seem to him materialistic. He objected solely on the ground that I ought not to be given permanent standing as a Lutheran minister until I had completed my course at Yale and the Synod could see how I turned out.

Fortunately, my father was present, having come to see me ordained. He was not then a member of the Allegheny Synod, but he had belonged to it for nine years and had been its president. He was given the privilege of the floor; and at the end of his plea for his son, there was only one vote against my ordination–that of the professor who had raised the objection. It chanced that he had been scheduled to deliver the ordination sermon, which he now refused to do. The officers of the Synod thereupon asked my father to take his place; he accepted the invitation, and I had the joy of being ordained with the laying on of his hands.

For the second of my three years as a student at Yale, I held the pastorate of the Bridgeport church, spending half of the week in Bridgeport and half in New Haven. I then resigned this church in order that it might have the services of a full-time minister.

The years at Yale were enriching. I reveled in the resources of the university library and even enjoyed writing papers for seminars. I read Aristotle's *Metaphysics* in the Greek with Dr. Stearns, and Schopenhauer's *Die Welt als Vorstellung* in the German with Dr. Montgomery; I studied the history of philosophy under Professor Duncan, and ethics under Professor Sneath; and I had courses and seminars in psychology, metaphysics, Kant's *Critiques*, and the philosophy of religion with Professor Ladd. I was appointed assistant in the Psychological Laboratory, then under the direction of Professor Charles H. Judd; and my work with him in experimental psychology afforded a training in the principles and methods of the natural sciences that I much needed, and for which I have never ceased to be grateful.

In his *Pragmatism*, William James remarked that the theistic philosophers like Ladd and Bowne must feel themselves rather tightly squeezed between the absolute idealists on the one side and the radical empiricists on the other. If Ladd ever felt so constricted, he gave no evidence of it. His teaching was not querulous, apologetic, or merely defensive. In football parlance, he chose to carry the ball himself rather than use his energies in stopping his opponents. A truer figure would be to say that he steadily advanced, like a well-equipped army, through territory lending itself to slow but inevitable conquest, through the areas of psychological investigation and philosophical reflection, which he had set himself to traverse in the comprehensive books that began with his *Elements of Physiological Psychology* in 1889 and concluded with the two-volume *Philosophy of Religion* in 1905. Undergraduates could not understand him and scoffed at his definition of psychology as the science of "states of consciousness *as such*"; but we graduate students found him a stimulating teacher and gained profound respect for his prodigious learning.

During the period of my work under his direction, Professor Ladd was engaged upon the writing of his *Philosophy of Religion.* We usually found him so occupied when any of us would knock upon the door of his office in Lawrence Hall. He sat, as he wrote, in an ample cane-seated rocking chair, one arm of which was enlarged to make a fairly good substitute for a desk. His detractors used to comment blithely that his books read as though they were composed in a rocking chair—a remark that we who were his friends would indignantly reject as slanderous and as evidence merely of their inability to understand him.

I had two courses with Ladd in the philosophy of religion and was a member of two seminars that he conducted in connection with these courses. One year he devoted to a general treatment of the subject, starting out with the data of what we would now call the history of religion and the study of comparative religion; the second year dealt with the philosophy of the Christian religion. I read Jastrow, Menzies, Tiele, Max Muller, Tyler, D'Alviella, Jevons, Reville, J. G. Frazer, Hatch's *Influence of Greek Ideas and Usages upon the Christian Church*, and A. D. White's *History of the Warfare of Science with Theology*—to name at random authors and titles of descriptive and historical works that come immediately to my memory; and on the philosophical side, John and Edward Caird, A. C. Praser, Bowne, Pfleiderer, Sabatier, Guyau's *Irreligion of the Future*, Balfour's *Defence of Philosophic Doubt* and *Foundations of Belief*, Orr's *Christian View of God and the World*, and Martineau's *Study of Religion.* I profited greatly by the study incidental to the writing of major papers for the seminars, especially one on the problem of evil and another on the meaning of revelation and inspiration.

The best work that I did with Ladd was in the study of Immanuel Kant. In a comparatively small seminar group, we devoted one year to the *Critique of Pure Reason* and the *Critique of Judgment.* I became so interested in Kant that I chose to write my dissertation upon some aspect of his philosophy; and I was directed by Professor Ladd to the fact that the full significance had not yet been explored of Benno Erdmann's discovery that the antinomy of reason rather than the issue between rationalism and empiricism was the real clue to the development of Kant's thought and the motive that led him to the principle of Criticism. I sent to Germany for a copy of Erdmann's

Reflexionen Kants zur Kritik der reinen Vernunft and other necessary materials, and went to work, with the result that after the usual despair and travail of soul, I finally completed a dissertation entitled *An Historical and Critical Study of Kant's Antinomy of Pure Reason.* It was one of the dissertations of that year that received a subvention from the university to help defray the cost of publication; but publication was not then required, and I felt that I wanted to work it over again before putting it into print. Then I began to teach–it is a not uncommon story–and got so occupied with my work that the revision was never completed. If anyone wishes to consult my doctoral dissertation–which no one has ever yet wished to do, so far as I know –he must ask to see the typewritten copy in the Yale Library.

I have never regretted devoting so much time to the study of Kant. I often suspect, when I read some glib reference to him, that the writer has not read the Critiques for himself and is merely turning over the common stock-in-trade of the textbooks. Kant's philosophy is not negative, but positive in intent. Faith was for him no last resort, no afterthought; the *Critique of Pure Reason* was meant to be followed by the *Critique of Practical Reason.* Grant as we must, that one hundred and fifty years of science, discovery, and invention have expanded the empirical content of knowledge far beyond anything that Kant could dream and that even mathematics is no longer as rigidly *a priori* as it was for him, it yet remains true that no reasoning that is based upon facts only can reach incontrovertible conclusions upon the one side or the other of the great issues concerning the ultimate character of reality; it remains true that philosophy must take account of man's moral nature, human obligations, ideals, and values; it remains true that with respect to God, freedom, and immortality, our minds are not coerced but that reasonably valid convictions are inevitably based in part upon the choice of attitude, conscious or unconscious, toward moral obligation that Kant calls faith. My colleague, Professor Macintosh, is far from a Kantian–and I personally believe that his realism is a truer account of knowledge than Kant's principle of faith.

The study of Kant's antinomies led me to certain articles in the *Revue de Metaphysique et de Morale*, and these in turn to Henri Poincare's *La Science et L'Hypothese.* Discussions on almost daily walks with John W. Withers, later dean of the School of Education of New York University, who was writing a dissertation on the philosophical implications of the non-Euclidian geometries, helped me to get the point of Poincare's discussion and to see how the works of Lobachevski and Riemann were undermining the rigid certainty of the mechanistic science of the nineteenth century. Although we did not know it at the time, we were looking from afar at the early stages of the movement that was destined to issue in the new physics and Einstein's theory of relativity.

I was not interested in mathematical physics, however, but in religion. And convictions that had begun to shape themselves in my mind as a result of the studies that I have described were sharply clarified when I read William James' *The Will to Believe.* The first five of these essays–particularly the first, which gives the title to the volume, and the fifth, on "The Dilemma of Determinism"–impressed me greatly. The title of the work is easily parodied, and much fun has been made of the wistful *wish* to believe or of the stouthearted, determined man who clenches his fists, gets red in the face, grits his teeth, and mutters, "I *will* believe." But criticism based upon such misconceptions of James's essay is as cheap as it is easy and does not affect the central truth of his discussion of the logic of faith. James was about as different from Kant as another philosopher could be. He was a radical empiricist, to whom Kant's rationalistic habits of thought and architectonic ways were anathema, and for whom the categorical imperative was simply a moral demand; yet the two men are not far apart in the place they give to faith.

There were things to be said on the other side, of course. I think I gave due consideration to them. While I worked on Kant, I was also reading Guyan and especially Schopenhauer, whose pessimism is the antithesis of Kant's faith. James's essay sent me to Huxley, who coined the term "agnosticism" so that he too could have a name and whose spirit of open-minded sincerity in the search for truth commanded my unqualified admiration, and to W. K. Clifford, whose *Ethics of Belief* is a clear, overconfident statement of positivism. Clifford's article was first published in the *Contemporary Review* for January 1877, and I found in the number of that magazine for the following June a reply bearing the same title by Professor Henry Wace, which is so pointed and so convincing that it ought to be reprinted and made generally accessible. Wace's discussion of the conditions of faith remarkably anticipates some of the conditions propounded in James's essay. "The object in moral matters," he says, "is to act, not only to act rightly, but to act promptly. . .while the object in matters of Science is to know, and to know accurately, and for that purpose to reserve a decision for as long a time as may be necessary." Clifford's "universal duty of questioning" would make the practical business of living impossible, for society can only exist upon a basis of mutual truth and faith. "Life was not made for men of science, but for men of action; and no man of action is good for anything if he cannot sometimes form a belief on insufficient evidence, and take a leap in the dark."

The general problem of the relations of knowledge and faith and concomitant problems of the mutual relations of science, morality, and religion have been so central in my thinking and so foremost in the intellectual life of the twentieth century that I am in danger here again of lapsing into bibliography. I mention merely a few recent books that I have read with profit: D. M. Baillie's *Faith in God and Its Christian Consummation*, B. H. Streeter's *Reality* and *Adventure*, the essays edited by Joseph Needham under the title *Science, Religion and Reality*, and William Adam Brown's *Pathways in Certainty*. I have been stimulated by the writings of A. N. Whitehead and by those of Henry H. Wieman, and I owe more to William Ernest Hocking than to any other of my contemporaries.

From about 1907 to 1910, in company with the general run of mankind, I had an attack of pragmatism. I read James, Peirce, Schiller, and Dewey assiduously and expounded the movement before various groups of folk who were curious about it, just as groups have since been curious about Coue's practice of autosuggestion, Watson's behaviorism, or Freud's psychoanalysis. But I never quite succumbed to pragmatism and in due time recovered, the principal remedies being my robust philosophical constitution, the writings of Josiah Royce, and the pointed little book by James B. Pratt entitled *What Is Pragmatism?*

John Dewey survived the passing of the vogue of pragmatism and became our most widely known philosopher. I have been most helped by his *Democracy and Education* and by *Ethics*, which he wrote in collaboration with Professor Tufts and which I used as a textbook with eight successive senior classes at Carleton. The "instrumentalism" in accordance with which he proposed that philosophy be reconstructed leaves me cold. Within my experience, notable extensions of the principles of scientific method to new fields have been made; and each such achievement is cause for rejoicing. We need all of the knowledge we can get, and we should hold our religious beliefs as well as our scientific hypotheses subject to revision in the light of further experience. But Dewey abolishes the "dualism" between science and morality, and achieves the triumph of "instrumentalism" only by an undue simplification of the problems involved in a theory of values and by arbitrarily ushering metaphysics and religion out of court. In his autobiographical account of his transition, "From Absolutism to Experimentalism," he associates his discarding of religious faith with personal experiences and gives as reason for his failure to discuss the problems of religion a fundamental conviction that the religious tendencies of men will always adapt themselves to any required intellectual change.

Whenever, on the last page or two of one of his books, Dewey hesitatingly refers to religion, he describes it as a sense of the possibilities of existence and devotion to the cause of these possibilities. One of his most sympathetic interpreters, Professor Wieman, has thus phrased it: "Religion consists in giving supreme devotion to the highest possibilities of value which the existing world can yield without knowing specifically what these possibilities are." Rather abstract and vague, a robust, adventurous, youthful sort of religion. We need its spirit.

I venture to think, however, that such a religion involves more than human self-confidence, more than the belief that the future holds possibilities of values yet unimagined. It involves a certain confidence in the structure of the universe itself, a certain metaphysical faith—a faith that this is the kind of universe in which values are bred that yields to honest effort, a universe in which values can be gained and kept, advances made and held. Just as science is possible only because, beneath all changes, it holds fast to the principle that nature is consistent and understandable, religion affirms that, beneath all mutations of human life and fluctuations of opinion, the universe is dependable. Meaning and value are there to be discovered; they are not merely self-confident projections of human desire.

From 1905 to 1916, I was professor of philosophy in Carleton College, in Northfield, Minnesota, and for five years of this period, dean of the college. I found Carleton an institution of about three hundred students, based upon the best New England tradition, and I shared in the early stages of the remarkable development that it experienced under the administration of Donald J. Cowling, who became its president in 1909. I taught psychology, using Angell's textbook and Seashore's manual of experiments, until the growth of the work led to the employment of a second teacher, to whom I surrendered this course. I started a department of education, which in due time was also handed over to someone else. I helped to train and place about four hundred graduates of Carleton as high school teachers; and in 1913, I was president of the Minnesota Educational Association.

My main interest, however, was the teaching of philosophy; and to my joy, nearly every student who did not drop by the wayside in their freshman or sophomore year, elected one or more courses in my department. The history of philosophy was my chief course, as I have always felt that this constitutes the best introduction to philosophy. Most students elected it, and throughout the year, they read Rogers' *Student's History of Philosophy*, some of the more important sources such as Descartes's *Meditations* and Berkeley's *Principles* in the convenient Open Court editions. William DeWitt Hyde's *From Epicurus to Christ* (republished as *Five Great Philosophies of Life*), Royce's *Spirit of Modern Philosophy*, and James's *Pragmatism* and *Will to Believe*. In ethics, as I have said, I used Dewey and Tufts and with these Royce's

Philosophy of Loyalty, a really great little book that ought to be more read than it is. In logic, we studied Hibben; and in the philosophy of religion, the students read the interesting combination of James's *Varieties of Religious Experience* and Royce's *Religious Aspect of Philosophy*. Textbooks and readings changed from time to time, of course, but the list I have given is of the books that lasted longest and that may serve to characterize the occupation of my mind in eleven happy years of teaching philosophy at Carleton.

In 1909, I was asked by the Lutheran Board of Publication to write for them a textbook for the training of Sunday school teachers. The work took all of the time I could spare from my classes for two years, and in 1911, the book was published with the title *The Pupil and the Teacher*. It chanced to be one of the first textbooks of a new type and began at once to sell widely, then later was incorporated into the first syndicated series of teacher-training textbooks issued in accordance with principles agreed upon by the Sunday School Council of Evangelical Denominations and the International Sunday School Association, which were soon to unite as the International Council of Religious Education. . . .

The years have brought increased responsibilities and multiplied contacts and have opened to me many opportunities for cooperative and interdenominational service. I have been since 1914 a member of the International Sunday School Lesson Committee and have served on many committees of the International Council of Religious Education, of whose Educational Commission I became chairman. Since 1917, I have been a director of the Congregational Education Society and the Congregational Publishing Society, and I have been for some years chairman of the Administrative Committee of the two societies. I became in 1924 chairman of the Commission on Christian Education of the Federal Council of Churches of Christ in America, and then chairman of the Administrative Committee of the Federal Council. Since 1928, I have been chairman of the Executive Committee of the World's Sunday School Association. An unforgettable and enriching experience was my sharing in the meeting of the International Missionary Council at Jerusalem for the two weeks prior to Easter, 1928. In 1929, I was elected chairman of the American Standard Bible Committee, a committee of fifteen scholars to whom was given the custody and control of the text of the American Standard Edition of the Revised Bible. This committee is undertaking a thorough revision of the American Standard Version, which it plans to release for publication in 1941, and I count my participation in this important work as one of my major tasks for the next ten years.

I have been honored by four theological seminaries with appointments to endowed lectureships, and I have fulfilled the duties of these appointments, except for my obligation, in one case, to publish the lectures. I have written several books, but one, which I hope will be my *magnum opus* based on the lectures just mentioned, is unfinished, and I shall not find time to complete it until I can take a sabbatical furlough. My primary interest, which is also my greatest enjoyment, remains what it always has been—the work of teaching. And I feel a certain justifiable pride in the students who have here come under my instruction—more than eight hundred ministers scattered through all the major Protestant denominations and sixty recipients of the higher graduate degrees, most of whom are professors of religious education in colleges and seminaries, while others hold high administrative posts with the International Council or related organizations.

I kept my connection with the General Synod of the Lutheran Church until 1916, although there was no English Lutheran Church for me to join in Northfield, Minnesota. I came to feel that it was wrong to remain without a local church membership, and my wife and I joined the Congregational church with which the college was associated. When we went to New Haven, I had gotten so occupied with various aspects of the work of the Congregational churches that it seemed wisest to retain that relationship, and I transferred my ministerial standing to the New Haven West Association of Congregational Churches and Ministers. This transfer involved no change in my theological views. I am glad that the freedom of the Congregational fellowship can embrace a Lutheran in theology.

Not that I care for party names. My years of teaching men who come from twenty to twenty-five denominations have made me tolerant of their differences of creed and polity and sensible of the common faith that undergirds them all. Our agreements are far more important than our differences. To be a Christian is the great thing and the hard thing.

Yet I have used a party name in the title of this autobiographical confession—"The Religious Education of a Protestant." That means not simply that I reject the dogma of papal infallibility, the doctrine of transubstantiation, and the system of sacramental penance. It means positively that I conceive and hold my Christian faith in the spirit of the Protestant Reformation. I sought to describe that spirit in an address before the students of the Yale Divinity School at the formal opening of one academic year. Let me conclude this personal confession by setting down here some of the things I then said.

Protestantism is democracy in religion. This does not mean that God is elected by popular vote or His kingdom liable to fickle revolution. It does not mean that all people are equally qualified to understand and declare His will. It does mean that Protestantism recognizes the right of all people to stand on their own feet before God, to obey their own consciences, and to determine their own beliefs in the light of what they deem to be the will of God. It affirms the right of individual judgment and the universal priesthood of believers. It believes that God is accessible to every soul that seeks Him, without the intermediation of ecclesiastical officialdom. It conceives the church as the congregation of believers and assumes that when people gather in groups to worship God or organize themselves for His service that the laws of social psychology operate in these as in all other human relationships.

Protestantism is concerned with our common life. It conceives religion not in terms of monastic cells, celibate vows, and withdrawals from the affairs of this world with a view to the accumulation of merit in the next but in terms of the fresh air, the wholesome affections, the common duties, and the homely responsibilities of this present world. Salvation, for the Protestant, is living in the power of the grace of God. Such salvation is possible here and now; one need not die to gain it. It lifts one out of meanness and pettiness, out of bondage by lust and fettering by habit to the levels of high affection and generous deed. For Luther, such salvation came as a joyous vision of the fatherly love of God; for Calvin, it was submission to His kingly decrees; but for both men, the old distinction between the sacred and the secular began to vanish. The will of God may be done on earth as in heaven. All life is sacred; every good calling is a divine vocation. All that humanism stands for, in positive affirmation and achievement, is normal to Protestantism.

Protestantism trusts the human mind. It believes in the competence of man to apprehend God, to respond to Him with faith, and to gain new insights and increase of power by the experimental method of basing activity upon such knowledge as we have and such faith as we dare venture. Grant, as we must, that the being of God lies beyond the power of our finite minds fully to grasp, comprehend, and formulate; grant, too, that these minds of ours are too commonly blinded by sin, biased by complexes, prejudiced by the traditions of yesterday, and cramped by the social pressures of today—yet these minds are the only minds we have. If we cannot trust them, we can trust nothing. Protestantism is realistic in its view of the human mind and awake to its failures and follies; yet it refuses to fall into scepticism or agnosticism. It insists that such minds can cope with the problems of value as well as matters of fact; that they can seek and find God as well as probe the laws of nature. Man's fallibility does not shut him out from saving faith in the infallible God or from growth in knowledge of God and of His will.

Protestantism believes in the divine initiative. Its God is not dead, but living; not absent, but here; not in passive hiding, waiting to be discovered, but active, disclosing Himself in every impulse toward goodness, beauty, and truth. Granting that all human analogies are but symbols of the exhaustless being of God, Protestantism yet affirms that the least inadequate symbols, the forms of thought and speech that most nearly approximate what we know and may believe about God, are drawn from the relations that ideally hold between parent and child. God is no mere king, or judge, or exacting creditor; He is a Father, loving, gracious, merciful, and infinitely patient.

Protestantism finds its most definite assurance of the divine fatherhood in the life and teaching, the death and resurrection of Him who most completely fulfilled His sonship to God–Jesus Christ. It is not merely as an ethical teacher or even as an example of what human life may be that Jesus Christ is the central figure in human history. It is because He is more than an historical figure. It is because He affords us a glimpse of ultimate Reality, because we see in Him the character and disposition of God dwelling among us, because God was in Christ reconciling the world unto Himself. That vision of God in Christ is the gospel of Protestantism; its evidence is the power that it has exerted throughout the centuries, and that it now has, to awaken conscience, to inspire love and trust, and to save us from folly and wrong. When we affirm belief in the living, eternal Christ, we declare our conviction that the character and disposition of God thus glimpsed is consistently true and forever dependable.

Protestantism is not an organization. It is a spirit; a way of thinking and living. To realize this gospel in my own life, and to equip young people to be its effective ministers, is my vocation.

2

TOWARD CHRISTIAN UNITY

In the first decade of the twentieth century, Carleton College was making, with dignity and grace, the transition from the long administration of its founder, President James W. Strong (1870 - 1903), to the even longer administration of President Donald J. Cowling (1909 - 45). Cowling and I had been fellow-students of philosophy in the Graduate School at Yale, and our work together at Carleton soon ripened into a close personal friendship. It was with a real tug of regret that I told him in the spring of 1916 that I had decided to accept the Horace Bushnell Professorship of Christian Nurture at the Divinity School of Yale University.

That decision was almost as great a surprise to me as it was to him. In the eleven years that I had been at Carleton, I had declined two college presidencies, and in the next eleven years at Yale, I declined three more, in each case on the ground that I chose to teach rather than to enter the field of college administration. I had also declined calls from other institutions to professorships of philosophy. One of these, from President George E. Vincent of the University of Minnesota, attracted me, but I felt that it would be disloyal to Carleton for me to move to its big neighbor just forty miles away.

Moreover, I was now a man with a family and with strong roots in Minnesota. On June 15, 1909, at her parents' home in Red Wing, I had married Clara Boxrud, a Carleton graduate in the class of 1907. With the aid of a loan from my father, I bought a house near the college, and in the home that we there established, two sons were born: Richard in 1912 and Luther in 1914. We were happy in our friendships and in my work. I could easily have been content to serve Carleton for as many years as President Strong had devoted to it or as many as Cowling was destined to be its president.

My father and mother and brother had come from Pennsylvania to be present at our wedding, and they remained as guests for a week in the hospitable home of Clara's parents, Richard and Jennie Boxrud. As befits bride and groom, Clara and I departed immediately on a honeymoon, first for a few days in Chicago, buying furniture, carpets, and the like in stores where we were warmly welcomed because we brought letters from Clara's father, who owned a department store in Red Wing. Then we went to Pennsylvania to visit first with my sister and her family in Reading and thereafter with my parents in Mechanicsburg, where I lectured at the Lutheran Summer Assembly, then in session at Irving College. In August, we returned to Minnesota, found our purchases awaiting our arrival, and had the joy of placing everything according to our hearts' desire in our new home. I then discovered what a prize I had won, for this student who had made excellent grades in her college courses was also an admirably competent cook and housekeeper.

That last sentence may seem to be unduly materialistic—as though good cooking and competent housekeeping were her primary assets. They were not. I had never thought of them before our marriage. I had fallen in love with a wonderfully gracious and radiant woman. She proved to be a loving and devoted mother as well, giving of herself unselfishly to our four children, the two sons born in Northfield, and two daughters, Margaret and Ruth, born in New Haven in 1916 and 1922. She was in truth the heart of the family and an inspiration to us all. I am devoutly thankful that we were granted more than fifty-five years of happy married life before her death on September 5, 1964.

Our closest friends in England have been Lord and Lady Mackintosh of Halifax. He died just after Christmas, 1964, and I have been reading his posthumously published autobiography, *By Faith and Work*, which Lady Mackintosh sent me as a Christmas present two years later. He has a statement concerning his wife that I want to quote because it applies as perfectly to Clara and myself as it does to Constance and Harold Mackintosh: "I never cease to marvel at my fortune in marriage. Usually in life things never turn out to be so good or so bad as we think they will, but as far as wives go, fate has turned out for me better than I could ever have dreamt of. Every page of my scrapbook of memory is lit by her presence and her smile. She is the same today as Viscountess Mackintosh of Halifax as when she was plain Mrs. Mackintosh. But then, of course, she was never plain Mrs. Mackintosh."

The Pupil and the Teacher

In the fall of 1909, I had received a letter from the Lutheran Publication Society informing me that they were planning to publish a four-volume series of textbooks for the training of Sunday school teachers and asking me to write the second volume of the series, to be entitled *The Pupil and the Teacher*. I was intrigued by the idea because this volume would deal with matters common to all denominations, while those that are distinctively Lutheran would be handled either in the first volume, *The Book and the Message*, or in the third and fourth, entitled *The School and the Church* and *The Lutheran Church and Child Nurture*. I accepted the invitation, and the book was published in 1911.

The Pupil and the Teacher soon became a best-seller. It was published not only by the Lutheran Publication Society for the use of its constituency but also for the general public by the George H. Doran Company, New York, and by Hodder and Stoughton, London. Imprint editions were published by various denominational publishing houses, in some cases with authorized additions or abridgements of their own. It was translated into Chinese, Japanese, Portuguese, and Spanish for use by missions and churches in lands where these were vernacular languages. New plates were needed in 1929, and a new edition was published, with a revised teaching apparatus and an up-to-date bibliography for each chapter. The book finally was permitted to go out-of-print in the 1940s. In all, well over a million copies had been sold.

Years later, the Yale News Bureau released a story concerning Yale's five "book millionaires," authors whose book sales had exceeded that figure. Here I was pleased to be included with Thornton Wilder, Robert Penn Warren, and two of my Divinity School colleagues, Roland Bainton and Kenneth Latourette. In actuality, the figure in my case now probably tops two million if one includes *Talks to Sunday School Teachers*, *Training of Children in the Christian Family*, *American Idealism* (volume X in *Pageant of America*), *Jesus and the Educational Method*, *We Are Able*, *The English New Testament from Tyndale to the Revised Standard Version*, *The Bible Word Book*, *The New Testament Octapla*, and *The Genesis Octapla*. Parenthetically, I might note that the cent-a-copy royalty that I received from my first book, *The Pupil and the Teacher*, enabled me to build the summer home at Lake Sunapee that gave the entire family such pleasure for some forty-five years.

The publication of *The Pupil and the Teacher* plunged me into the movement toward better religious education. I was made a member of the Commission on Religious and Moral Education appointed by the National Council of the Congregational Churches, and I drafted the survey of "The Present Status of Religious Education in Congregational Churches," which it presented in a sixty-five page *Report* submitted to the meeting of the Council at New Haven in October 1915. I became a member of the Religious Education Association, then in its pristine vigor with Henry F. Cope as general secretary. I attended the International Sunday School Convention at Chicago, in June 1914, at which a new charter was devised for the International Sunday School Lesson Committee, and I was elected as a member of the committee under that charter.

The Religious Education Association had been founded in 1903 by a nationwide group of educators, led by President William Rainey Harper of the University of Chicago, President James B. Angell of the University of Michigan, President Henry Churchill King of Oberlin College, and Chancellor James H. Kirkland of Vanderbilt University –to name only four of a long list of men and women engaged in the work of education at every level. An organization of individuals of various religious affiliations, it declared its purpose to be threefold: "To inspire the educational forces of our country with the religious ideal, and to keep before the public mind the ideal of religious education, and the sense of its need and value." The Religious Education Association was interested in churches and Sunday schools, of course, as well as in colleges, public schools, private schools, and all other agencies and means of education. I had found the annual volumes of its *Proceedings* a rich mine of experience and suggestion as I explored the field in preparation for writing my book. I have kept my membership in the Religious Education Association throughout the years; and I was glad to be associated with Rabbi Abba Hillel Silver of Cleveland and President Paul C. Reinert, S.J., of St. Louis University when each of us gave one of the three addresses on "The Crisis of Religion in Education," at the opening assembly of the Golden Anniversary Convention of the Religious Education Association, held at the University of Pittsburgh, November 10-12, 1953.

The International Sunday School Lessons

The term "International" as applied to the International Sunday School Lesson Committee stands for the representation of Canada as well as the United States in its membership and service. From 1890 on, there was a measure of correspondence and cooperation with a British Section, but this ended with the formation of the British Lessons Council in 1915. The first International Sunday School Lesson Committee was appointed in 1872 for a term of six years, and successor committees were elected in every sixth year thereafter. These usually consisted of fifteen members. The bylaws of the International Sunday School Association in 1911 defined the powers and duties of the Lesson Committee to be: "to select from the Holy Bible the weekly lessons, the golden texts, the daily readings, determine the titles, and issue the same without further interpretation."

The outstanding characteristic of these lessons is that they were "uniform," that is, intended for the use of all teachers and pupils of the Sunday school, young and old. Such uniformity created problems –especially for the teachers of children. I remember that one of my friends told me how he and his wife were awakened to a weakness of the plan when they entered their young son in the primary class of the Sunday school and found that the lesson for the day was about whose wife a woman would be in the resurrection when she had married seven men. The date was September 16, 1906; the lesson was Mark 12:13-27, and its subject was "Jesus Silences the Pharisees and Sadducees."

The heyday of the International Uniform Sunday School Lessons was in the 1890s and early 1900s. At the beginning of that period, these lessons were used by more than ten million teachers and pupils; twenty years later, by double that number.

But the Uniform Sunday School Lesson system had grave defects. The lessons were not adapted to the understanding or the needs of the pupil; they contained no principle of progression and lacked connection with the rest of the pupil's education; and they failed to give a coherent view of the Bible as a whole or of the progressive revelation that it records. Lesson "helps" were provided in the form of paperbound quarterlies, but the use of these tended to replace the direct use of the Bible; and the editors, having formed an Editorial Association in 1901, went so far as to recommend that, if larger passages of Scripture are chosen for study, "the part names for printing be indicated as the less" and that this "be limited to about ten or twelve verses where possible."

The International Sunday School Lesson Committee was not unaware of these defects but opposed the limitation of the lessons to ten or twelve verses. It sought, from 1896 on, to meet the needs of various age groups by issuing "optional" outlines of lessons for beginners, for pupils in the primary classes, and for advanced courses for adults; but these met with little success.

Meanwhile, the movement toward a completely graded system of lessons gathered strength. In 1906, a Graded Lesson Conference was organized under the leadership of Mrs. J. W. Barnes, Elementary Superintendent on the staff of the International Sunday School Association, who had obtained the consent of its Executive Committee to take this step. The members of this conference were teachers in active service; they met monthly for more than two years, engaged in the preparation of graded lesson outlines. They enlisted the interest and help of some of the denominational publishing houses, notably the Methodist, Presbyterian, and Congregational. And they offered the results of their work to the International Sunday School Lesson Committee in the hope that it would be found helpful.

On January 2-3, 1908, the chairman of the Executive Committee of the International Sunday School Association presided at a conference of fifty-four men and women whom he had invited as representatives of the Lesson Committee, the Editorial Association, the Graded Lesson Conference, and the Executive Committee. This conference resulted in the unanimous adoption of the following resolutions:

(1) That the system of a general lesson for the whole school, which has been in successful use for thirty-five years, is still the most practicable and effective system for the great majority of the Sunday-schools of North America. Because of its past accomplishments, its present usefulness, and its future possibilities, we recommend its continuance and its fullest development.

(2) That the need for a graded system of lessons is expressed by so many Sunday-schools and workers that it should be adequately met by the International Sunday-school Association, and that the Lesson Committee should be instructed by the next International Convention, to be held in Louisville, Ky., June 18-23, 1908, to continue the preparation of a thoroughly graded course covering the entire range of the Sunday-school.

These resolutions were unanimously adopted by the Lesson Committee and by the convention. The committee found the prior work of the Graded Lesson Conference to be of great help as it proceeded to prepare the outlines for the International Sunday School Lessons: Graded Series, which it began to release in January 1909. Textbooks for these lessons were published by a syndicate of Methodist, Presbyterian, and Congregational publishing houses, as well as by the American Baptist Publication Society and other denominational publishers.

I was, of course, committed to the principle of graded lessons; and I was glad to find, in the survey of the status of religious education in Congregational churches that I drafted in 1915, that two-thirds of the reported Sunday schools were using the Graded Lessons.

In 1910, a new organization entered the field, the Sunday School Council of Evangelical Denominations, a mark of the more definite assumption by the Protestant denominations in the United States and Canada of responsibility for the educational work of their Sunday schools and for the training of teachers. The new charter for the International Sunday School Lesson Committee, which was devised in 1914, expressed an agreement reached by this new organization and the older International Sunday School Association. It enlarged the Lesson Committee to consist of eight representatives of the International Sunday School Association, eight representatives of the Sunday School Council of Evangelical Denominations, and one representative from each denomination maintaining a distinct board or committee for the oversight and welfare of its Sunday schools. In 1922, the Sunday School Council of Evangelical Denominations and the International

Sunday School Association merged to form one organization known as the International Council of Religious Education, under which the charter of the Lesson Committee remained unchanged until 1928. In 1928, its responsibilities were included among those assigned to a newly organized Educational Commission, and the International Sunday School Lesson Committee, after fifty-six years of service, was discontinued.

I was a member of the Lesson Committee from 1914 to 1928 and thereafter served for two four-year terms as chairman of the Educational Commission. My most important assignment as a member of the Lesson Committee was to serve as chairman of a Commission of Seven of its members, appointed by it in 1920 "to undertake a thorough survey of the lesson situation in the light of the experience of those using the courses now in existence; and in the light of this survey, to make recommendations concerning the future policy of the International Sunday School Lesson Committee." Two years were devoted to the studies and conferences entailed in this survey. The final report of the Commission of Seven, submitted April 20, 1922, recommended that the Graded Series, now completed, be released to the denominations for such publication, with or without revision as they might desire. For the future policy of the Lesson Committee, it recommended (1) the continuance of the Uniform Lessons, with such adaptions to departmental use as may be called for; (2) the preparation of "a new series of Group Graded Lessons, Biblical in content, dated, and running through three-year cycles for the several age groups"; and (3) the creation of "an entirely new curriculum, to be known as the International Curriculum of Religious Education, to provide an integrated curriculum for Sunday and weekday hours, and to be based upon the latest developments of educational theory and practice."

The future lay, in my judgment, with the third of these recommendations. It was in line with the conception of the Sunday school to which I had committed myself in *The Pupil and the Teacher*, especially in the chapters on "Grades," "The Class as a Social Institution," and "The Spiritual Goal." It soon became clear, however, that there could be no such entity as *the* International Curriculum of Religious Education, and the decision was reached that "the work of the International Council in the curriculum field is not primarily that of producing materials for use in local churches but of developing principles and procedures by which to guide the many curriculum enterprises now under way."

In the fifty years since that decision was reached, the curricular service of the International Council of Religious Education and its successor, the Division of Christian Education of the National Council of the Churches of Christ in the U.S.A., has been remarkably effective. Outstanding contributions at various stages have been made by Paul H. Vieth, Mary Alice Jones, and Gerald E. Knoff, Yale alumni whom I had counseled in their graduate study for the Ph.D. degree. My personal share was to serve as chairman of the Committee on Basic Philosophy and Policy, whose report was adopted and published in 1940 under the title *Christian Education Today*. At present, the Department of Educational Development is serving, with equal effectiveness, those who still cherish the "uniform" plan and those who are engaged in the development of more comprehensive and vital curricula of Christian education.

3

THIRTY-FOUR YEARS OF SERVICE AT YALE

In 1910, under the leadership of Dean Edward L. Curtis, the faculty of the Yale Divinity School had adopted a new curriculum, organized in four departments, each directed toward a specific type of Christian ministry. These were: (1) pastoral service; (2) missions; (3) religious education; and (4) practical philanthropy. In the catalogue for 1912-13 and thereafter, "practical philanthropy" was replaced by "social service." The aim of the department of religious education is stated as "to prepare men to teach the Bible and to give religious instruction in colleges, and to serve as directors of religious education in the churches; also to prepare students for leadership in the educational work of Young Men's Christian Associations." This catalogue lists E. Hershey Sneath as professor of the philosophy of religion and of religious education, offering courses in the psychology and philosophy of religion, psychology of adolescence, principles and methods of religious education, and a religious education seminar for advanced students. Other courses in Yale College and the Yale Graduate School that were open to students in the department were taught by Charles F. Kent, history and methods of religious education; by Arnold Gesell, principles of education and educational hygiene; by Ernest Carroll Moore, methods of study and the course of study, history of education, school administration, the hygiene of child development; and by Edward Cameron, educational psychology.

Sneath, a graduate of the Yale Divinity School, B.D. 1884, and of the Yale Graduate School, Ph.D. 1889, had been a member of the fac-

The excerpts on pages 41-44 are taken first from *Beyond the Ranges* by Kenneth Latourette, reprinted here by permission of the publisher, William B. Eerdmans Publishing Co., and second from *Yale and the Ministry* by Roland Bainton, used here by permission of Harper and Row, Publishers.

ulty of philosophy in Yale College from 1889 on, attaining the rank of professor of philosophy in 1898. His major interest was in ethics, and he had as early as 1891 offered a course in "pedagogics." As a teacher of philosophy to undergraduates, he was interesting, clear in exposition, and understandable. In 1912, he accepted the invitation of the faculty of the Divinity School to become one of its members and to undertake the development of the department of religious education.

With the help of Charles R. Brown, who had become dean in 1911, Professor Sneath obtained the gifts that endowed the Stephen Merrell Clement Professorship of Christian Methods, the Horace Bushnell Professorship of Christian Nurture, and the Shattuck and Samuel Thorne Lectureships in Religious Education. By their own gift, he and Mrs. Sneath later established the Richard Sheldon Sneath Memorial Library of Religious Education in memory of their son. He also obtained the gift of the Samuel B. Sneath Memorial Publication Fund, which provided for the publication of meritorious researches carried on under the direction of the faculty of the Divinity School, especially in the field of religious education.

For the first of the new professorships, there was no doubt who should be chosen. It was Henry B. Wright, then assistant professor of history in Yale College, and a remarkably gifted leader in the religious life of the students–indeed, the endowment of the Clement Professorship had been made with the knowledge of the donors that Henry Wright would be invited to accept it.

For the other professorship, there was no such immediate prospect. Professor Sneath read my book *The Pupil and the Teacher*, remembered me as one of his former students, and wrote to me, suggesting that if I could take a sabbatical year from my work at Carleton College the faculty of the Divinity School would appoint me as a lecturer on religious education for that year, offering a general course on principles and methods of religious education and a more advanced seminar. I took this letter to President Cowling and told him that after nine years of service I would welcome such a sabbatical year; and he, as another Yale graduate, agreed. So I accepted Professor Sneath's proposal, and Clara and I, with our two young sons, spent the academic year 1914-15 in New Haven as one of the faculty families of the Divinity School.

As a student in the Graduate School from 1902 to 1905, I had known little about the Divinity School, which was then at the lowest ebb in its history. But when I returned in 1914, I found it to be a live, growing institution. A regeneration had been brought about under the effective leadership of Edward L. Curtis, dean from 1905 until his death in 1911, and Charles R. Brown, who succeeded him. I thoroughly enjoyed teaching the two courses for which I was responsible as a lecturer.

President Cowling had promised to relieve me of the deanship of Carleton College, which I had held since 1910, so that I returned to Carleton with the happy prospect of a schedule of teaching unhampered by administrative duties. But in the spring of 1916, I received a letter from Dean Brown informing me that Mrs. Dotha Bushnell Hillyer had made a gift endowing the Horace Bushnell Professorship of Christian Nurture in memory of her father, and he invited me to accept appointment as the first incumbent of the new chair. So I was faced with a major decision. I had already put aside all thoughts of college administration in favor of teaching. Now I decided that my vocation should be in theological education at the graduate level, and I accepted the invitation from Yale. I entered upon more than three decades of service as a member of the faculty of Yale University until I retired as Sterling Professor of Religious Education and Dean of the Divinity School, Emeritus, in June 1949.

I am glad to record that my decision involved no straining of old friendships. Carleton College conferred upon me, as a parting gift, the honorary degree of Doctor of Divinity. My friendship with Cowling remained unbroken, and we were frequently associated in the ensuing years. My son Richard was a member of the Carleton faculty for three years, from 1939 to 1942, leaving to serve as an officer of the United States Army Air Corps in India and China during World War II. I returned to Carleton to deliver the Phi Beta Kappa oration in 1939 and to deliver the commencement address in 1945, when Cowling was about to retire and his successor, Laurence Gould, had been chosen. On the latter occasion, Cowling linked our names with characteristic diplomacy and grace, saying, "If I were asked to name the four or five best teachers that Carleton has had during the past thirty-six years, two of them would be Luther Weigle and Larry Gould."

Until 1923-24, the professorial team of the Yale department of religious education consisted of Sneath, Wright, and myself. We were aided in 1916-18 by Benjamin S. Winchester, assistant professor, who came to us from the editorship of the Sunday school publications of the Congregational churches and left us to become educational secretary of the Federal Council of Churches. In the 1920s, we were aided by a young instructor in historical theology, Robert L. Calhoun, who soon became one of Yale's outstanding teachers and finally Sterling Professor of Historical Theology. We had also the assistance of part-time lecturers, drawn from the staff of the New Haven Young Men's Christian Association and compensated by the income of the Shattuck and Thorne funds. I find that I published in the *Yale Divinity News*,

May 1923, an article concerning Professor Sneath's prospective retirement that contains a statement concerning the student enrollment as follows: "Affiliation with the department of education in the Graduate School throws open to our students the list of courses offered by the faculty of that department. Practically all students of the Divinity School elect one or more courses in religious education before graduation; and the enrollment of students at present majoring in religious education numbers forty-five candidates for the B.D. degree, eight candidates for the M.A. degree, and ten candidates for the Ph.D. degree."

The retirement of Professor Sneath in June 1923 and the untimely death of Professor Henry Wright in the following December led to new appointments. Robert Seneca Smith, professor of Biblical literature at Smith College, came to us as visiting professor of religious education for two years, 1923-25. In June 1924, I was made Sterling Professor of Religious Education, and in 1925, Smith succeeded me as Horace Bushnell Professor of Christian Nurture. Henry Wright's field was assigned to Clarence Shedd, who began his notable career as lecturer in fulfillment of the provisions of the Stephen Merrell Clement endowment. He became assistant professor in 1926, associate professor in 1929, and professor in 1939. From 1920 on, the resources of the department of religious education were greatly enhanced by the establishment of a new department of education in the Graduate School, the courses of which were open to our students. This made available to them a faculty that came to include Frank E. Spaulding, Samuel Brownell, J. Crosby Chapman, George S. Counts, Bessie L. Gambrill, Charles T. Loram, Clyde M. Hill, Mark May, John S. Brubacher, and Warren Tilton, to name only those whose courses were most often elected by our students in the thirty-seven years of this department's existence.

In 1930, Hugh Hartshorne joined us as research associate with the rank of professor, serving also as liaison with Yale's newly founded Institute of Human Relations. When I went to China in January 1935, I asked Hartshorne to teach the course in the psychology of religion that I had been conducting since Sneath's retirement. When I returned from China in September of that year, I found Hartshorne ready to retain this field, so I did not resume it; and in 1951, Hartshorne's title was changed to professor of the psychology of religion.

Robert Seneca Smith died in January 1939 and was succeeded in the Bushnell Professorship by Paul H. Vieth, a graduate of the Divinity School in the class of 1924 and of the Yale Graduate School, Ph.D. 1928. He had served as general secretary of the Missouri Sunday School Council before entering the Divinity School, had been director of religious education at the Church of the Redeemer while a student at

Yale, and from 1925 to 1931 was director of research and superintendent of educational administration for the International Council of Religious Education. In 1931, we had brought him back to the Divinity School as director of field work and associate professor of religious education. His doctoral dissertation had been published in 1930 by Harper & Brothers under the title *Objectives in Religious Education*. He now passed on the directorship of field work to Ralph L. Woodward and devoted full time to service as the Horace Bushnell Professor of Christian Nurture. He served in Japan as adviser on religious education to the Supreme Command Allied Powers, 1947. And he returned to Tokyo as a Fulbright scholar to teach in the International Christian University in 1954-55. He retired in 1963, and the Bushnell Professorship was conferred upon Randolph C. Miller, who had succeeded me as professor of religious education upon my retirement in 1949.

I had made it a condition of my acceptance of the Bushnell Professorship in 1916 that I should have standing in the faculty of the Graduate School and freedom to develop graduate study in the field of religious education leading to candidacy for the Ph.D. degree. This was approved by all concerned, and I was welcomed as a member of the department of philosophy, of which Charles M. Bakewell was then chairman. This assignment was natural and unquestioned, for all courses in the study of education that were offered at Yale from 1891 to 1920 were under the aegis of the department of philosophy. When Ernest Carroll Moore was called in 1910 from the superintendency of the public schools of Los Angeles to a professorship at Yale, the title given him was professor of education in the department of philosophy, psychology, and education. Moore left in 1914 to go to Harvard and later returned to Los Angeles, where he was destined to have a notable career. When I became a member of the department of philosophy in 1916, I found myself associated with two other professors of about my age, Edward Cameron, in educational psychology, and Arnold Gesell, who was beginning his remarkable lifetime work in the study of child development and hygiene.

In the closing years of his administration, President Arthur T. Hadley was much interested in the idea of establishing a strong department of education in the Graduate School. His concern was shared by the secretary of the university, Anson Phelps Stokes, who wished Yale to take part in furthering the great tradition of public education initiated by Horace Mann and Henry Barnard. When the question was raised with the department of philosophy, Gesell and I were asked to explore the possible lines of action. We reported in favor of a reorganization of the study of education at Yale, to take the form not of a separate school of education but of another independent and coordinate department in the Graduate School–incidentally, the study of psychology was destined for similar status. The department of philosophy approved and so recommended to President Hadley, who then obtained the approval of the Yale Corporation. In his last presidential report, President Hadley expressed the hope with which the new department of education was established: "Yale will probably never be a place for a very large teachers' college. Its situation in a city of moderate size, while it is good for much of its regular work, puts it at some disadvantage in this respect. But it can and should be a place to which teachers of the country will look for the same kind of leadership that we have already assumed in law and in medicine, in music and in forestry."

The department of education in the Graduate School was organized and began its work in 1920, under the chairmanship of Frank E. Spaulding, who was succeeded in 1929 by Clyde M. Hill. From the beginning, the cooperation between the department of education in the Graduate School and the department of religious education in the Divinity School was cordial and effective. We of the Divinity School relied upon the Graduate School department for courses in educational psychology and in the history, philosophy, and administration of public education, while they of the Graduate School welcomed our participation in the general seminar, which was a basic part of their program. Seneca Smith and Hugh Hartshorne attended this seminar regularly and carried their full share of its work; Shedd, Vieth, and I attended it occasionally, when some topic called for our presence and service. At the invitation of Professor Hill, Hartshorne, Smith and I contributed chapters to the book entitled, *Educational Progress and School Administration*, which was published in tribute to Professor Frank E. Spaulding on his retirement, containing chapters by twenty-one of his former colleagues.

Throughout my period of active service, 1916-1949, the Divinity School's department of religious education had direct access to the committees of the Graduate School in charge of recommendations for the higher degrees. We made a good beginning, for the first Ph.D. dissertation written under my direction was awarded the five hundred dollar John Addison Porter prize at commencement in June 1921. It was by George Stewart, entitled "A History of Religious Education in Connecticut to the Middle of the Nineteenth Century." Incidentally, it brought me in touch with one of Yale's great American historians, Charles M. Andrews, to whose friendship and counsel I owe a great deal. During the 1920s, I served for some years as a member of the committee for Ph.D. degrees in the humanistic studies–a pleasant duty from which I was naturally excused after I became dean of the Divinity School in 1928.

Just before my retirement in June 1949, I wrote to one of our Ph.D. alumni in answer to a question: "I have cast up the figures and find that ninety-three students have received the Ph.D. degree through the department of religious education. Of these, fifty are now college or theological seminary professors; twelve are college or theological seminary presidents; five are denominational officers in the field of religious education; thirteen are interdenominational officers in some service of the general cooperative movement of the churches; and thirteen are parish ministers. The group of interdenominational officers would, of course, be considerably widened if we add to it those who have taken their Ph.D. here at Yale in other departments, such as Forrest C. Weir, and those who have taken the B.D. but have not gone on for the Ph.D., such as Roy G. Ross. I take great pride in these students who have earned their degrees at Yale and gone out into places of high responsibility and influence in the cooperative movement among the churches."

After my retirement, the supervision of graduate study in religious education was committed, with other fields, to the department of religious studies, and in the past twenty years, thirty Ph.D. dissertations have been accepted that could formerly have been under the aegis of the department of religious education. A heavy blow was sustained in the 1950s when the department of education in the Graduate School was abolished, and Yale experimented with a Master of Arts in Teaching (MAT) program. But as I write this, in December 1969, the current number of the *Yale Alumni Magazine* brings the news that this program is to be discontinued as "no longer making a distinctive contribution to public school education."

The Deanship of the Yale Divinity School

In 1928, I became dean of the Divinity School, and in 1931, what Professor Bainton has called "the great quarter of a century" began. Fortunately, we have accounts by both of the well-known historians who were members of the faculty. I shall quote first from the autobiography of Kenneth Latourette, entitled *Beyond the Ranges*, and then from the last chapter of Roland Bainton's *Yale and the Ministry*. Latourette's account is more personal, reflecting current interest; Bainton's is quite objective, based upon the records.

Latourette's account:

After my first ten years on the Yale faculty the environment under which I lived changed drastically, although by stages, both physically and in personal relations. Shortly before the close of the decade Dean Brown became emeritus and was succeeded by Luther Weigle. Dean Brown was a noted preacher and that, when he came to the Divinity School, was much needed. He markedly increased the enrollment and attracted a denominationally more varied student body. Dean Weigle had many gifts. In addition to being a great teacher, he was an educator, a scholar of varied and eminent attainments, and a superb administrator. He quickly stiffened the standards of admission. For a time this reduced the attendance, but it distinctly augmented the quality of the student body. He also added to the faculty, bringing on it such men as Robert Calhoun and Richard Niebuhr. The better standards and the fame of the young, promising faculty eventually brought even more students than before he came into office.

Physically the environment was completely altered. In the summer of 1931 the buildings which had been erected for the Divinity School between fifty and sixty years earlier were razed to make way for Calhoun College, one of the ten new undergraduate colleges which were erected in a revolutionary change in Yale's undergraduate housing. Money and the site had been obtained for a much enlarged plan for the School, but it would not be ready for occupancy until the autumn of 1932. In the twelve months' interval the School was housed in Hendrie Hall, formerly used by the Law School, and adjacent former residences owned by the University were assigned as dormitories.

The new Divinity School Quadrangle was one of the early achievements of Dean Weigle. By wise negotiations he had obtained a grant from the Sterling trustees for its erection and equipment. After World War I the estate of John W. Sterling had come to Yale. Sterling was a graduate of Yale College, a New York lawyer, and a bachelor. By wise investments he had acquired a fortune from which Yale eventually received about thirty million dollars. By his will most of his estate was to go to Yale. He did not give it directly, but appointed as trustees a group of his friends to whom, with some restrictions, was left the decision as to how it was to be spent. The will directed that an important building be erected as a memorial. That, at the request of the University authorities, the trustees decided should be the Library, greatly needed, and in due course it was constructed. The College and the Law and Medical Schools were given buildings. Ample endowments were provided for Sterling professorships which, at the decision of the President, were to be given to outstanding scholars on the faculty to encourage and aid research. The trustees declined to assign one to the Divinity School. President Angell obtained one for Weigle on the ground that the latter's chair was religious education, and in approaching the trustees stressed education.

Dean Weigle went to Anson Stokes, father of the future bishop, who was a clergyman and had been Secretary of the University for more than twenty years. Mr. Stokes had talked repeatedly with Mr. Sterling about his plans for Yale and said that the latter was deeply interested in religion, but wished it to be nonsectarian. Dean Weigle pointed out that the Divinity School met that requirement, for, like the University, while originally Congregational, for several decades, along with the University as a whole, it had been officially declared to be undenominational. His request was given additional weight by the fact that, through Professor Tweedy's characteristically quiet initiative the Rockefellers had promised a million dollars to the Divinity School on condition that it be matched from other sources. The Divinity School received a share of the twenty million dollar fund then being raised by Yale, and the Sterling trustees agreed to provide for the erection and maintenance of the Sterling Divinity Quadrangle.

The site first assigned for the new quadrangle was not far from the center of the University, a plot facing Hillhouse Avenue and occupied by two residences which belonged to Yale. The tenant of one of these houses was highly indignant at having to move and by her protests embarrassed the administration. The architect had drawn preliminary plans for the new building when a much larger site on the crest of a hill further from the University center became available through the death of the owner. George P. Day, the Treasurer of the University, to whom the occupant of the originally assigned site had repeatedly complained, obtained an option on the other site, explained the situation to the faculty of the Divinity School, and the latter voted to endorse the change. Fortunately construction had not yet begun. The architect's plans were adjusted and enlarged to meet the new situation and in the year 1931-32 the quadrangle bearing the Sterling name was erected. In the course of the years the change proved advantageous. The enrollment of the Divinity School grew beyond what had been anticipated and the site originally assigned would have cramped the School. In their later years I was glad to thank both the protesting woman and George Day for the change.

Bainton's account:

The last quarter of a century has been the greatest in the history of the Yale Divinity School. The period has known two deans. Luther Weigle served for twenty-one years, from 1928 to 1949, when he was succeeded by Liston Pope. The selection of these two men was indicative of a new emphasis. Both were taken, not from the parish ministry, but from the ranks of the teaching profession. Both were already serving on the faculty. At the time of Brown's coming, the decision to call an eminent minister was wise, but in 1928 the need was to raise the educational standards of the school to a par with the other departments of the University.

Dean Weigle and President Angell embarked with hearty accord on this endeavor. The President agreed that the School should share fully in the resources of the University and like other departments might operate on a deficit budget. The Divinity School had endowments of its own and Dean Brown had felt obligated to live within their income, but the assumption throughout the University came to be that expansion and the equalization of departments should be financed from general funds. In these the Divinity School was to share, as well as in enlarged benefactions. Five hundred thousand came from the University campaign, a million from John D. Rockefeller, Jr., and two and a half million from the Sterling trustees.

These gifts made possible the new Sterling Divinity Quadrangle on Prospect Street. The old buildings on College and Elm, once heralded as "a permanent habitation," had long since been antiquated, and the site was desired by the University for Calhoun College. The summit of Prospect Street afforded grounds sufficiently spacious for the buildings then to be constructed and for the expansion ultimately contemplated. In Georgian Colonial, a style simple and functional, dormitories were provided for the unmarried men and buildings for administration and teaching in addition to a refectory, gymnasium, library, and a chapel chaste and worshipful.

The School, thus handsomely treated by the University, set out to measure up to all of the educational requirements of the institution. Entering students were required to have a B.A. degree and could receive no advanced standing by reason of work done in college. Henceforth students were not to be recruited but attracted by the reputation of the School. The time had come when this step might be ventured because Brown's recruitment had started the flow of a continuing stream and the alumni of the School in churches and colleges already constituted a recruiting agency. Dean Weigle's step was so abundantly justified that in 1930 the decision was reached to limit the enrollment and to practice selective admission. Since then, sometimes one-third and sometimes even one-half of the applicants have had to be denied. The maximum enrollment has advanced, however, from three hundred to four hundred.

In 1931 in the interest of higher educational standards the curriculum was revised and the number of courses taken by a student at a given time was reduced. Prior to Dean Weigle's administration, the student normally took eight courses of two hours each; the year was divided into two semesters. This scheme was replaced by three terms and the normal load came to be four courses with the hours in class variable. Language courses met four times a week, lecture courses three, and seminars two. By this arrangement the student might have as few as eight hours a week in class and seldom more than fourteen. Under Dean Pope the semester plan has been restored in order to conform to the schedule of the University, but the restriction of the courses to four and the flexibility as to hours in class have been retained.

One result of these measures has been to introduce a greater stability into the student body. Whereas previously a high percentage of the students stayed only for one year, the more stringent educational demands persuaded them of the necessity of three continuous years. From 1925 to 1931 the average annual enrollment was two hundred thirty-three of whom only ninety-nine were returning students, whereas from 1931 to 1941, with practically the same enrollment, the average number of those returning was one hundred forty-two. The student body under the selective process is of the highest quality, both academically and in every other regard. In 1932 women were admitted as candidates for the B.D. degree. Since that time they have numbered about 10 per cent. In academic performance the women are above the average of the school.

. . .The student body is derived not primarily from the indigent or the affluent but from the middle brackets with a goodly number from the ranks of the professions. Commonly forty-three states are represented and sometimes as many as sixteen foreign countries. The number of colleges of which the students are graduates numbers as high as two hundred twenty-three. . . . The number of denominations fluctuates at around thirty-four. . . . The very complexion of the School makes a great contribution to the ecumenical movement. There is not much shifting of denominational allegiances by reason of this mingling, but there is an advance in mutual understanding and respect.

4

FOUR LONG-TERM CHAIRMANSHIPS

Like others of active temperament, I have chaired, from time to time, various committees, boards, or associations. Four of these appointments have been of exceptional duration and importance. They were as chairman of the executive committee of the American Association of Theological Schools, 1928-48; chairman of the executive committee of the World's Sunday School Association, 1928-58; chairman of the committee of scholars that produced the Revised Standard Version of the Bible, 1930-66; and chairman of the planning committee for the National Council of the Churches of Christ in the U.S.A., 1941-50.

American Association of Theological Seminaries

The movement toward cooperation among theological seminaries began in a modest way in August of 1918, when, at the invitation of President Lowell, delegates from fifty-three seminaries and colleges in the United States and Canada met at Harvard University. Published findings of the Conference were quite properly meager. Its substantial result lay in the appointment of a Continuation Committee empowered to call another conference and authorized to organize committees for the study of various problems and interests common to the institutions engaged in the education of candidates for the Christian ministry.

To supplement the information in this chapter, three outside accounts have been added. The compiler thanks Dr. Gerald E. Knoff, former Executive Secretary, Division of Christian Education of the National Council of Churches, for his account of Luther Weigle's service to the World's Sunday School Association and his account of Luther Weigle's role in the planning for the establishment of the National Council of Churches. The account of the work of the Standard Bible Committee was written by Luther Weigle for the *Festschrift* honoring Professor Herbert Gordon May on the occasion of his retirement from Oberlin College in 1970 The *Festschrift* was published that year under the title *Translating and Understanding the Old Testament*, edited by Harry T. Frank and William L. Reed. Portions which appear in brackets indicate material added by Luther Weigle for clarity.

Subsequent Conferences were held biennially: in 1920, at Princeton; 1922, Toronto; 1924, Garrett Biblical Institute; 1926; Yale; 1928, Union Theological Seminary, New York; 1930, Chicago; 1932, Gettysburg; and 1934, Colgate-Rochester. At the tenth biennial meeting, held at Crozer Theological Seminary in 1936, a new constitution was adopted, and the Conference became the American Association of Theological Seminaries. It was at the 1928 meeting that I became chairman of the Executive Committee of the Conference, six years later to become the Association.

Outstanding among the projects undertaken during this chairmanship was the comprehensive study of theological education made by the Institute of Social and Religious Research upon the initiative of the Conference. Dr. Robert L. Kelly had made a survey of 161 theological schools in the United States and Canada in 1924 under the institute's auspices, but the main result had been to stimulate interest in a much more thorough and complete study. The institute was prevailed upon to appropriate the necessary funds, and Dr. Mark A. May was appointed director of the study. Launched on June 1, 1929, the study was published in 1934 in the four volumes entitled *The Education of American Ministers*.

The Conference of 1934, held at Colgate-Rochester, came after the published volumes had appeared, and seminary faculties had had several months in which to read and digest them. After full discussion, it was decided to appoint three commissions for the ensuing biennium: one on Standards of Admission; one on Accrediting Institutions of Theological Education; and one on Cooperation, including consideration of possible reorganization of the Conference itself. The Executive Committee was authorized, "in view of the complexity of the problems assigned to these Commissions. . .to seek a gift of funds for the more effective prosecution of their work, and to employ such competent personnel as the receipt of funds may justify."

Even though funds did not materialize, it seemed best to go ahead with the appointment of an Executive Secretary to serve without salary. Dean Lewis J. Sherrill, of the Louisville Presbyterian Seminary, had so commended himself to the Conference by his chairing of the Committee on Curriculum, faculty personnel, and related subjects that he was the unanimous choice for the post. He accepted the call, and Louisville Seminary graciously afforded to the Conference a share of his time without compensation. The 1936 meeting at Crozer was of crucial importance. Dean Sherrill made his first report as Executive Secretary. Reports were adopted on preseminary studies and on standards of admission. A plan of accrediting theological institutions was initiated, and standards were adopted to guide the Accrediting Commission. The constitution of the Conference was revised, and the organization became the American Association of Theological Schools.

In 1953, I wrote hopefully of the Association's well-devised plans for a new comprehensive study of theological education because data obtained for *The Education of American Ministers* was then twenty-five years old. Great progress had been made in enhancing the state of theological education in this country, but much was yet to be done. In my opinion, the theological seminaries of the United States and Canada bear a tremendous responsibility, in the present state of the world, for the continued existence and welfare of sound theological education and Biblical scholarship.

The World's Sunday School Association

The long service of Dean Weigle to the World Council of Christian Education, formerly the World's Sunday School Association, was an important contribution to what later came to be called the ecumenical movement. His activities have been largely unnoticed in this country outside of a small group of colleagues. They deserve to be remembered as an expression of a concern for world-wide Christian education on the part of one whose influence, through his writing and leadership, extended to many nations and continents.

The agency had been founded as a result of the initiative of representatives of the Sunday School movements of the United States and Great Britain in the latter part of the 19th century. A joint call for a world convention was issued by the International Sunday School Association (United States and Canada) and the London Sunday School Union, and the first World Convention was held in London in early July, 1889.

Conventions were held thereafter at regular intervals, meeting in Great Britain, North America, Europe, the Near East, and Asia. Headquarters were in London and New York. A formal organization replaced the earlier joint cooperative sponsorship in 1907.

It was at the Ninth Convention held in Glasgow in 1924 that Professor Weigle first became involved with the organization. Sailing on the S.S. *Cameronia* from New York, Dr. Weigle gave three addresses on Christian education during the crossing, and preached at the ship's Sunday service on June 17th.

The Glasgow convention heard him present a scholarly report on the International Uniform Lessons, pointing out the inadequacies of this curriculum for the churches, a system which was, however, widely used. Though criticism of the lesson system had been made before,

Weigle's address was the first solidly documented critique, and set many churches and national bodies at work to devise a better plan for Christian teaching.

The Glasgow convention, recognizing his ability, elected this "first-timer" its Chairman, and he served in this capacity until 1958, a 34-year period of distinguished service. The Convention also elected as its President, Sir (later Viscount) Harold Mackintosh and thus began a warm friendship which continued until the latter's death in 1964.

As the World Council of Churches began its work, cordial relations and effective working relationships were established from its beginning in Amsterdam in 1948. Especially in youth work this fraternal relationship flourished. Dr. Weigle, who had been a delegate to the Utrecht conference which drew plans for the World Council of Churches, worked for, encouraged, and strengthened these joint efforts. After the term of his chairmanship had expired, he gave consistent support to the work of a joint Commission on education, established by the two bodies. When the two agencies consummated a complete merger in 1971, it met with his warm approval.

Dr. Weigle's popular book, *The Pupil and the Teacher*, and his long service as Chairman of the World Council of Christian Education made him known and loved in Christian churches around the world. He has been a significant pioneer. Along with his intellectual and administrative achievements, he has been deeply loved.

The Standard Bible Committee

The American Standard Version of the Bible, a variant of the Revised Version of 1881-1885, was published by Thomas Nelson & Sons in 1901, and copyrighted to protect the text from unauthorized changes. In 1928 the copyright was transferred to the International Council of Religious Education, a body in which the educational boards of forty of the major Protestant denominations of the United States and Canada were associated. That body appointed an American Standard Bible Committee of scholars to have charge of the text, and authorized it to undertake further revision if deemed necessary. The charter of the Committee contains the provision that "all changes in the text shall be agreed upon by a two-thirds vote of the total membership of the Committee"–a more conservative rule than had governed revision hitherto, which required only a two-thirds vote of members present.

[The members of this Committee were William P. Armstrong, of Princeton Theological Seminary; Julius A. Bewer and James Moffatt, of Union Theological Seminary; Henry J. Cadbury and James H. Ropes, of Harvard University; Federal C. Eiselen, of Garrett Biblical Institute; Edgar J. Goodspeed and J.M. Powis Smith, of the University of Chicago;

Alexander R. Gordon, of United Theological College, of Montreal; James A. Montgomery, of the University of Pennsylvania; A.T. Robertson and John R. Sampey, of the Southern Baptist Theological Seminary at Louisville; Andrew Sledd of Emory University; Charles C. Torrey and Luther A. Weigle, of Yale University. Professor Gordon died soon after the first meeting of the Committee, and in his place was chosen William R. Taylor, of the University of Toronto.]

The work of the American Standard Bible Committee was begun in 1930; it was suspended in 1932 because of lack of funds to provide for the expense of travel and secretarial service for the comprehensive revision which it decided to undertake. In 1937 the necessary budget was provided, and the revision proceeded, with the authorization of the following vote of the International Council of Religious Education: "There is need for a version which embodies the best results of modern scholarship as to the meaning of the Scriptures, and expresses this meaning in English diction which is designed for use in public and private worship and preserves those qualities which have given to the King James Version a supreme place in English literature. We, therefore, define the task of the American Standard Bible Committee to be that of revision of the present American Standard Bible in the light of the results of modern scholarship, this revision to be designed for use in public and private worship, and to be in the direction of the simple, classic English style of the King James Version."

The Committee worked in two Sections, one dealing with the Old Testament and one with the New Testament. In the experimental period, 1930-1932, five meetings, each of two or three days' duration, were held in New York. At the first of these Luther A. Weigle was elected chairman of the Committee, and the officers of the Sections were chosen: for the Old Testament, John R. Sampey as chairman and F.C. Eiselen as secretary; for the New Testament, James H. Ropes as chairman and Henry J. Cadbury as secretary. When the decision was reached in 1932 to recommend that revision of the American Standard Version be undertaken, Ropes dissented and resigned, and when the work began in 1937 Sampey asked that he be replaced by Kyle Yates, his associate on the faculty of the Southern Baptist Theological Seminary at Lousiville. So the practice of having separate chairmen for the Sections lapsed, the meetings of the Sections were scheduled at separate times and places, and Luther A. Weigle, as chairman, and James Moffatt, as executive secretary, were officers and voting members of both Sections. [Moffatt served until his death in 1944 while I continued active work for forty years, until my ninetieth birthday in 1970.]

. . .[As the Committee prepared to take up the work for which it was commissioned by the Council, there were several changes in membership. Of the original members only Bewer, Cadbury, Goodspeed, Moffatt, Taylor, and Weigle were left. To these were added in 1937 and 1938, Walter Russell Bowie, then Rector of Grace Church, New York; Millar Burrows and George Dahl, of Yale University; Clarence T. Craig, of Oberlin; Frederick C. Grant, of Seabury Western Theological Seminary; William A. Irwin, of the University of Chicago; Willard L. Sperry, of Harvard University; Abdel Ross Wentz, of the Lutheran Theological Seminary at Gettysburg; and Kyle M. Yates, of the Southern Baptist Theological Seminary at Louisville.] It should be stated that Bowie, Sperry, Wentz, and Weigle were members chosen under the provision contained in the action of the Council which established the Committee: "that not less than three and not more than five of the fifteen members of the Committee be chosen with a view to their competence in English literature, or their experience in the conduct of public worship or in religious education." The other members, six in each Section, were chosen for their competence in Biblical scholarship. Sperry was assigned to the Old Testament Section, Bowie and Wentz to the New Testament Section.

With the Committee was associated an Advisory Board of representatives chosen by each of the forty denominations affiliated with the International Council of Religious Education. The members of this Board were consulted with respect to the principles underlying the revision; they were afforded opportunity to review and make suggestions concerning the drafts of the work in progress.

The New Testament Section convened thirty-one times in the six years, 1937-1943, in meetings covering one hundred and forty-five days, with sessions scheduled from 9 A.M. to noon, 2:30 to 5:30 P.M., and 7:30 to 9:30 P.M. The meetings were usually at Union Theological Seminary in New York, at the Yale Divinity School in New Haven, or in the summers at the Northfield Hotel, East Northfield, Massachusetts. For a week in June 1938, and again for two weeks in the summer of 1939, we met as the guests of Professor and Mrs. Edgar J. Goodspeed at their summer home on Paradise Island, Plum Lake, Sayner, Wisconsin.

The initial draft of the revision of each of the books of the New Testament was prepared by one or two members of the Section, to whom it was assigned. This draft was then typed, and a copy sent to each member of the Section, for study prior to the meeting at which it would be considered. It was then discussed, verse by verse, in sessions of the Section. A new draft, prepared by Dr. Moffatt, in the light of the decisions then reached, was mimeographed and distributed for further study. At subsequent sessions of the Section, these mimeographed drafts were again discussed, verse by verse, and suggestions submitted by members of the Advisory Board and others were considered. A revised set of the mimeographed drafts was then submitted to the members of the Old Testament Section, who were given opportunity to record their dissent from any proposed change. At a meeting held in Northfield, August 15-29, 1943, the typescript of the entire New Testament was once more reviewed and the votes and comments of the members of the Old Testament were considered. The revised typescript was then placed in the hands of a smaller editorial committee, charged to prepare it for the press and supervise its publication, which took place on February 11, 1946.

Meanwhile, we had suffered our greatest loss in the death of Professor James Moffatt on June 27, 1944. A scholar of rare judgment and learning, he brought to the work of both Sections the rich resources of his training and experience as a translator and the genius and devotion of a really great soul. It is a matter of regret that there is no chapter by Moffatt in the seventy-two page paperbound *Introduction to the Revised Standard Version of the New Testament,* which was also published in February, 1946, containing essays by each of the other members of the New Testament Section.

The work of the Old Testament Section had proceeded along similar lines, though more slowly. At the meeting held in New York, June 14-30, 1943, Millar Burrows was added to this group, attending every session and assuming a full share thereafter of the work upon the revision of the Old Testament. In 1945 this Section was substantially reinforced by the election of five new members of the Committee: William F. Albright, J. Philip Hyatt, Herbert G. May, James Muilenburg, and Harry M. Orlinsky. In 1947 one more member was added in the person of Fleming James, who made his home in New Haven and became executive secretary of the Old Testament Section.

In 1937-1944 sixteen meetings of the Old Testament Section had been held; in 1945-1951, with the added membership, there were twenty-six meetings. In the earlier period, three meetings were at the University of Michigan, Ann Arbor; the other meetings of that period and all meetings of the later period were at Union Theological Seminary, the Yale Divinity School, or the Northfield Hotel. In all, the Old Testament Section held forty-two meetings, covering three hundred and fifty-two days; twelve of these meetings were of two weeks or more. The Revised Standard Version of the Bible, containing the Old and New Testaments, was published on September 30, 1952.

On the same date was published a ninety-two page paperbound *Introduction to the Revised Standard Version of the Old Testament*, containing essays by eleven members of the Old Testament Section and edited by its chairman. Again, it is a matter of regret that there are no chapters by William R. Taylor, who had been chiefly responsible for the translation of the Psalms but died on February 24, 1951, or by Julius A. Bewer, who had been an active member of the Committee from its beginning until the completion of its work but was now suffering from what was destined to be his last illness.

In response to the request of the General Convention of the Protestant Episcopal Church, October, 1952, the Division of Christian Education of the National Council of the Churches of Christ in the U.S.A., into which the International Council of Religious Education had merged, organized a committee of scholars to undertake revision of the English translation of the Apocrypha; its publication was authorized by the General Board, NCCCUSA, December 12, 1952. The scholars accepting this assignment were Millar Burrows, Henry J. Cadbury, Clarence T. Craig, Floyd V. Filson, Frederick C. Grant, Bruce M. Metzger, Robert H. Pfeiffer, Allan P. Wikgren, and Luther A. Weigle, who was appointed chairman. Five of these scholars were already members of the Standard Bible Committee, and the other four were promptly recognized as members, assigned to their appropriate Section.

A great loss was sustained in the death, August 20, 1953, of Dean Craig. In 1954, J. Carter Swaim became Executive Director of the Department of the English Bible, in the Division of Christian Education, and was added to the membership of this Committee.

The work involved the preparation and circulation of mimeographed drafts of translation, the discussion and resolution of all disputed points in face-to-face conference, the circulation of new drafts embodying the decisions reached in conference, and a final review of each book in the light of written agenda proposed by the members of the Committee and of the Advisory Board made up of representatives appointed by denominations which accepted the invitation to review the drafts. This procedure was similar to that followed by the Committee which prepared the Revised Standard Version of the Bible, containing the Old and New Testaments; and, in general, similar principles of translation were followed.

Meetings of the Apocrypha Committee were held at the Yale Divinity School January 30-31, June 22 to July 3, and December 18-23, in 1953; and December 7-9, 1956. Most of the conferences, however, were held at the Hotel Northfield, East Northfield, Massachusetts, where the Committee was in session over the following periods: August 17-19, 1953; June 14-26 and August 16-28, 1954; June 13-25 and August 15-27, 1955; and June 11-23, 1956.

The Revised Standard Version of the Apocrypha was published in 1957. The preface states that "No attempt has been made to provide introductions to the various books of the Apocrypha, as here translated. The scholar will not need them, and for the general reader there are admirable recent books on the Apocrypha by Charles C. Torrey, Edgar J. Goodspeed, Robert H. Pfeiffer, and Bruce M. Metzger. We gladly acknowledge our debt, not only to the scholars who throughout the centuries have made competent studies of these books, but also to the former English translations, especially the King James Version of 1611, the English Revised Version of 1895, and Goodspeed's translation of 1938."

The purpose of the Standard Bible Committee and the assignment of responsibility are stated as follows in the memorandum dated November 23, 1953, signed by Gerald E. Knoff and Luther A. Weigle: "The purpose of the Committee is:

"1. To have charge of the text of the American Standard Version of the Bible, and the revised Standard Version of the Bible.

"2. To recommend to the Division when, in its judgment, revision of the texts of these Versions should be made, or any other projects in the translation of the Bible or related books from the ancient languages should be undertaken.

"3. To make such revisions or new translations as may be authorized by the Council upon recommendation of the Division.

"It is understood:

"(1) That the copyright of the American Standard Version, the Revised Standard Version, and all revisions or new translations made by the Committee are the property of the Division.

"(2) That responsibility to determine the wording of the text of these versions, revisions, or new translations rests solely upon the Committee.

"(3) That responsibility for the budget of the Committee, for authorization of work to be undertaken by the Committee, for publication, and general policy, rests solely upon the Division."

Throughout the work of translation, 1937-1956, the Standard Bible Committee met by Sections, at dates so arranged that the chairman of the Committee could attend and serve as chairman of each of the Sections.

Since the completion of the translations, the work of the Standard Bible Committee has been done largely by correspondence, publication, and conference with interested parties such as, to cite notable examples: the Advisory Committee on English Bible Versions appointed by the Lutheran Church-Missouri Synod, and the committee of scholars representing the Catholic Biblical Association of Great Britain.

A general meeting of the Standard Bible Committee was held at Union Theological Seminary, New York, December 30, 1954, to consider the proposal of the Catholic Biblical Association of Great Britain.

The proposal was approved, and the Committee on the Apocrypha was authorized to consider and to grant permission for the changes in the text of the Revised Standard Version of the New Testament requested by the editorial committee of the Catholic Biblical Association of Great Britain. This was done by the Committee on the Apocrypha at its meeting in Northfield, June 25, 1955.

A general meeting of the Standard Bible Committee was held at the Yale Divinity School, June 9-16, 1959. This had been preceded by a mail vote upon an extensive agenda made up of criticisms and suggestions submitted by various readers from 1952 to 1959 which were of sufficient plausibility to warrant consideration by the Committee. As a result of this mail vote and the decisions reached in the eight-day meeting, a few corrections and changes in the text of the Revised Standard Version were authorized, a list of which was sent to each of the licensed publishers on October 1, 1959. Thomas Nelson & Sons made these corrections and changes in 1960, and the other publishers incorporated them in all editions, beginning September 30, 1962. These changes are described in a new paragraph inserted toward the close of the Preface, which reads as follows:

"These principles were reaffirmed by the Committee in 1959, in connection with a study of criticisms and suggestions from various readers. As a result, a few changes have been authorized for the present and subsequent editions. Most of these are corrections of punctuation, capitalization, or footnotes. Some changes of words or phrases are made in the interest of consistency, clarity or accuracy of translation. Examples of such changes are 'from,' Job 19.26; 'bread,' Matthew 7.9, 1 Corinthians 10.17; 'is he,' Matthew 21.9 and parallels; 'the *S*on,' Matthew 27.54, Mark 15.39; 'ask nothing of me,' John 16.23; 'for this life only,' 1 Corinthians 15.19; 'the husband of one wife,' 1Timothy 3.2, 12; 5.9; Titus 1.6."

In 1960 ten new members were elected to the Standard Bible Committee: (1) as Old Testament scholars, Raymond A. Bowman, Frank M. Cross, Robert C. Dentan, Marvin H. Pope, Alfred von Rohr Sauer; (2) as New Testament scholars, Francis W. Beare, Sherman E. Johnson, John Knox; (3) chosen for competence in English literature, the conduct of public worship, or Christian education, Theodore O. Wedel, Amos N. Wilder.

A general meeting of the Standard Bible Committee was held at the Yale Divinity School, June 16-19, 1965, with sixteen members present. The agenda was based upon correspondence during the preceding six years, upon the careful study of the Revised Standard Version of the Old Testament by Millar Burrows, and upon items submitted by Herbert G. May.

It was understood that the Committee has no authority to make changes at the present time, since we are pledged to the publishers to leave the text unchanged for ten years. Yet substantial progress was made in rejecting many items upon the agenda, in definitely assigning other items to one of the Sections or to individual members for study and report, and in recording present approval of other items while recognizing that no such approval can be regarded as final.

There was general agreement that the Committee should plan to meet in 1968 and at two-year intervals thereafter, and general agreement that the Revised Standard Version is so important, as the representative in our time of the Tyndale-King James tradition and as a bridge linking Catholic and Protestant, that it must not be dealt with hastily. If and when the time comes that further revision should be desirable, in the judgment of the Standard Bible Committee, it will follow the procedure outlined in the paragraphs of the memorandum which has been quoted.

On May 3, 1966, the Catholic Edition of the Revised Standard Version of the Bible was published in Edinburgh and London, followed on July 1, 1966, by its publication in America and Australia. The preparation and publication of this edition are a Catholic project, undertaken at Catholic initiative, edited by Catholic scholars, and bearing the approval of the Catholic Church. It is a Catholic project with which the Standard Bible Committee and the Division of Christian Education are gladly cooperating.

A full account of the project, from its inception in 1953 until the present, has been published by Father Reginald Fuller, D.D., of the Catholic Biblical Association of Great Britain, editor of the Catholic Edition of the Revised Standard Version of the Bible, in his Introduction to the published volumes and in articles which he wrote for publication in *The Tablet*, London, and in the *Catholic Ecumenical Review* which now bears the name *One in Christ*. The article in the second of these publications is entitled, "The Revised Standard Version Catholic Edition and Its Ecumenical Significance."

On May 26, 1966, the *New York Times* carried a front-page article with the news that Richard Cardinal Cushing, Archbishop of Boston, had given his official *imprimatur* to The Oxford Annotated Bible with the Apocrypha. This is an important addition to the approvals already given for the use of the Catholic Edition of the Revised Standard Version of the Bible.

The Oxford Annotated Bible was first published in 1962 by the Oxford University Press. The Revised Standard Version is used as its text, and it is equipped with general and special introductory articles, extensive annotations at the bottom of each page, and a new set of maps. The editors are Dr. Herbert G. May, Professor of Old Testament, Oberlin Graduate School of Theology, and Dr. Bruce M. Metzger, Professor of New Testament, Princeton Theological Seminary. This volume immediately won praise and wide use, especially by ministers and by students in colleges, universities, and theological seminaries. One Catholic college, the Jesuit College of the Holy Cross in Worcester, Massachusetts, promptly adopted it as the required text for all its Biblical courses. In 1965 the Oxford University Press produced the Oxford Annotated Apocrypha, and later in that year the two volumes were published together as the Oxford Annotated Bible with the Apocrypha.

Because of a growing acceptance of this volume in Catholic circles, the Oxford University Press decided to approach Cardinal Cushing for his formal approval of this edition of the Bible. He expressed his willingness to consider the request if a joint committee of Catholic and Protestant scholars reviewed the matter and made recommendations. This committee consisted of Father Philip J. King, Professor of Sacred Scriptures, St. John's Seminary, Boston, and Father W. Van Etten Casey, S. J., Professor of Theology, Holy Cross College, Worcester, Massachusetts, who, together with Father Eugene H. Maly, Mt. St. Mary's Seminary of the West, Norwood, Ohio, consulted with the editors, Dr. May and Dr. Metzger.

This informal committee reached full agreement on all details. They decided that no changes were desirable or necessary in the text or footnotes of the Revised Standard Version or in the general or special introductory articles except for that upon Ecclesiastes. A few minor changes were made in the annotations. These consisted chiefly of adding a brief explanation to particular phrases or verses to indicate where the Catholic interpretation differs from the Protestant interpretation.

Two weeks after the committee submitted its recommendations, Cardinal Cushing granted his endorsement in the form of an *imprimatur* to the Oxford Annotated Bible with the Apocrypha. He also expressed his "pleasure to be associated with this ecumenical venture which should have far-reaching fruitful results."

In my judgment, the far-reaching fruitful results which Cardinal Cushing envisages are assured in due time. The two avenues toward common use of the Revised Standard Version of the Bible by Catholics and Protestants are complementary and mutually reinforcing, rather than competitive. Catholic Edition is a part of the copyrighted title of the edition of the Revised Standard Version prepared by the Catholic Biblical Association of Great Britain with our consent. No other edition can use that title, which was proposed at the conference in London, 1954, when Dom Bernard Orchard, O.S.B., the Reverend Reginald C. Fuller, D.D., L.S.S., and their associates met with Dr. Peter Morrison, Dr. Gerald E. Knoff, and myself. The decision to adopt it and go ahead with the project was easily reached by the Standard Bible Committee and the Division of Christian Education; but ten years of hard work to perfect the plan, to surmount opposition, and to secure ecclesiastical approval lay before Fathers Orchard and Fuller. The present approval of the Oxford Annotated Bible with the Aprocrypha rests largely upon their success. We must not forget that Cardinal Cushing wrote the Foreword for the American printing of the Catholic Edition of the Revised Standard Version of the Bible, as well as granted the *imprimatur* for the Oxford Annotated Bible with the Apocrypha: Revised Standard Version.

These two volumes are complementary for two reasons. One is that they are of a different scope; the Catholic Edition is simply a Bible, with only the brief explanatory notes which canon law requires, while the Oxford Annotated affords ample help to the student of the Bible. The other reason is that the difference between the two volumes clearly pinpoints the major differences that remain between Catholic and Protestant views of the Scriptures. These are concerned with the canon of the Old Testament, and with the degree to which Catholic usage and doctrine should be reflected in the New Testament. I have no doubt that in due time, Catholics and Protestants will come to closer agreement with respect to these matters, but there is no good to be gained by undue hurry. And in the meantime, it is good that both Catholics and Protestants should be kept aware of these differences and of how small they are in comparison with the great truths which we hold in common.

At the annual meeting of the Program Board of the Division of Christian Education, February, 1966, Paul S. Minear was elected to membership in the Standard Bible Committee, assigned to the New Testament Section, and Herbert G. May was elected as chairman of the Committee. Professor May accepted this post with the understanding that he would not devote full time to it until his retirement in 1970 from the faculty of Oberlin College, and that until then Luther A. Weigle would continue in active service as vice-chairman of the Committee in charge of its office at the Yale Divinity School.

A six-day meeting of the Standard Bible Committee was held at the Yale Divinity School, June 17-22, 1968, attended by seventeen members, under the chairmanship of Professor Herbert G. May.

This meeting was of special significance because it was the first meeting of the Standard Bible Committee to engage the presence and participation of Roman Catholic biblical scholars. Hitherto, our cooperation with Catholic scholars has been by conferences and correspondence. But at the meeting in June, 1968, three Catholic scholars were present, not as observers or conferees, but as participants with full freedom of initiative and discussion and with right to vote. They were invited with the approval of the RSV Policies Committee and the Program Board of the Division of Christian Education. They and three others who could not be present at this meeting were nominated by an *ad hoc* committee composed of Professor May, Dean Weigle, Dr. Knoff, Professor Metzger, and Professor Minear.

Dean Weigle introduced and welcomed to the Committee the Catholic participants from Great Britain (Dom Bernard Orchard and Dr. Reginald Fuller) and Canada (Professor David M. Stanley), and expressed the regrets of the Catholic scholars from the United States who were unable to be present at this meeting. There was a general discussion of Catholic participation in the Revised Standard Version of the Bible. Fathers Orchard and Fuller described their experiences in connection with the Catholic Edition of the Revised Standard Version; Professor Paul Minear gave a description of the service of investiture of Dr. Weigle into the Knighthood of St. Gregory the Great; and Professor Bruce Metzger reported on the granting of an *imprimatur* to the Oxford Annotated Bible with the Apocrypha.

The problem of a "You-Your" edition of the Psalms and of the entire RSV Bible was discussed. It was the sentiment of the Committee that now was not the time to make a decision, for the liturgical practices closer to the time of the publication of an updated Revised Standard Version should be taken into consideration. Perhaps by 1976 the situation will be clearer. It was recognized that the "You-Your" forms were becoming increasingly popular, and that a different situation may face us in 1976 than that which caused the original decision of the RSV Policies Committee to grant permission for such changes only in response to application from a specific publisher, for specific passages intended for liturgical use, and only if opportunity is given for review of the text by a subcommittee, comprising Drs. May, Weigle, Wedel, and Wilder.

Substantial progress was made in dealing with the extensive agenda, both in plenary sessions of the Committee and in separate sessions of the Old Testament Section and the New Testament Section. In addition to suggestions arising from Professor Millar Burrows' thorough study of the RSV Old Testament, we had before us a body of suggestions arising in connection with Professor Burton H. Throckmorton's editing of the recently published Third Edition of his Gospel Parallels. There were also suggestions arising from the growing use of the Revised Standard Version by Catholics; suggestions made by a study committee of the Lutheran Church-Missouri Synod; suggestions made by a similar study of the Christian Reformed Church; besides questions and suggestions contained in letters of individual correspondents from June 1965 to June 1968. The Committee made plans to meet again in 1970, 1972, 1974, and 1976.

The six Roman Catholic Biblical scholars who were elected by the Program Board to the membership of the Standard Bible Committee are:

Dom Bernard Orchard, O.S.B., St. Benedict's School, Ealing, London, England
The Reverend Reginald Fuller, D.D., St. Mary's College, Twickenham, Middlesex, England
The Reverend Professor David M. Stanley, S.J., Regis College, Willowdale, Ontario, Canada
The Reverend Professor Joseph A. Fitzmyer, S.J., Woodstock College, Woodstock, Maryland
The Reverend Professor John L. McKenzie, S.J., University of Notre Dame, Notre Dame, Indiana
The Reverend Professor Eugene H. Maly, S.S.D., Mt. St. Mary's Seminary, Norwood, Ohio

I do not undertake to list or describe the outstanding contributions which Professor Herbert G. May has made to the editing and the growing use of the Revised Standard Version of the Bible since he became a member of the Standard Bible Committee [in 1945] . . . .When my advancing years made it advisable that a new chairman be chosen for the Standard Bible Committee, Professor May was a natural choice. The decision of the nominating committee was unanimous, and he was elected chairman in 1966. I rejoice in his acceptance of the responsibility that I carried for so long, and I have high hope for the future service of the Revised Standard Version of the Bible, under his leadership of the Standard Bible Committee, in the new ecumenical climate of the years that lie ahead.

The National Council of Churches

The National Council of the Churches of Christ in the United States of America is a comparatively young agency as ecclesiastical bodies go. It was founded in 1950 as a merger of twelve inter-church agencies, serving the communions of the United States and Canada.

With the absorption of these independent councils, the newly formed National Council of Churches began as a representative body of United States churches, twenty-six in number, all of them Protestant.

It received into its membership two years later, the Greek Archdioceses of North and South America, an Orthodox communion which was followed shortly by several other Eastern Orthodox bodies.

Each of these merging Councils had a tradition of service all its own, several of them going back into the 19th century, each with executive staffs, and defined areas of work, and, in some instances, world-wide services and personnel. Bringing them together was no easy, no simple task.

Nine of the agencies had appointed a joint committee to initiate this venture, and in April, 1941, the committee had chosen Dean Weigle to serve as Chairman, with Dr. Hermann Morse of the Presbyterian Church in the U.S.A. as Secretary.

The joint committee came to have several names in time, but through the successive changes Drs. Weigle and Morse remained its principal officers. A revised draft of a constitution was presented to the interdenominational bodies, and through them to their constituent bodies in the churches. In January of 1950 the approvals of the agencies were secured, and over a period of six years, the official governing units of the denominations were considering the completed plan of union, together with their intended relation to it. October of that year saw this process completed. In Cleveland, in the midst of a crippling snowstorm on November 29, 1950, the National Council of Churches, as it was usually called, was officially established.

During all this time, Dean Weigle served as the effective Chairman of the Planning Committee, the final name of the organizing committee. He was admirably suited for this task. For many years he had been an able leader in the International Council of Religious Education, serving that body as Chairman of its Educational Commission and Chairman of its Standard Bible Committee. He was active in the International Council's concerns in curriculum, weekday religious education, religion in public schools and other fields of work. Because of his long term chairmanship of the World Council of Christian Education, he was familiar with the educational work of churches in other lands. He had been President of the Federal Council of Churches from 1940 to 1942, eventful years in the life of the nation, studded with many troublesome issues between the nation and its churches. His twenty years of service to the Conference of Theological Seminaries gave him an intimate acquaintance with American and Canadian theological education. It is difficult to imagine another person in the early 1940s who had an equal breadth and depth of experience in the work of the churches.

As Chairman he was fair, irenic, and firm in keeping church executives and other representatives at their appointed tasks. It would not be true to say that he was always patient. "Usually," but not "always."

Progress was not always steady, and Dean Weigle, conscious of the desired goal to be reached, was not disposed to tolerate prolonged indecision. A colleague remembers one occasion, when a unit had procrastinated, changed direction, made commitments, qualified them, and then expressed its desire for time for further study. With a characteristic downward chopping motion of his right hand and arm, he exclaimed with obvious annoyance, "Can't these people ever make up their minds!" The unit finally did, and the Planning Committee got on with its job.

If today any one individual can be called the father of the National Council of Churches–and to be sure, it is the creation of many minds–Luther Weigle is that person.

5

THE REVISED STANDARD VERSION OF THE BIBLE

A notable service has been rendered by the International Council of Religious Education and its successor, the Division of Christian Education of the National Council of the Churches of Christ in the U.S.A. in their initiation and sponsorship of the Revised Standard Version of the Bible. The vote of the Council, authorizing the Standard Bible Committee to proceed with the work of revision, directed that the resulting version should "embody the best results of modern scholarship as to the meaning of the Scriptures, and express this meaning in English diction which is designed for use in public and private worship and preserves those qualities which have given to the King James Version a supreme place in English literature."

The King James Version, published in 1611, was itself a revision of prior English translations, beginning with those by William Tyndale, published in 1525-35. Tyndale set the basic structure for the translation of the Bible from Hebrew and Greek into English, which has endured through all subsequent changes. Next to Tyndale, the King James Version owes much to Coverdale, 1535-39; the Geneva Bible, 1560; and the Rheims New Testament, 1582. It was itself a direct revision of the Bishops' Bible, 1568-1602 and owes to this some of its faults as well as some of its virtues. In general, it kept felicitous renderings from whatever source, which had stood the test of public usage.

The King James Version had to compete with the Geneva Bible. For seventy years after its publication, it endured bitter attacks. It was denounced as theologically unsound and ecclesiastically biased, as truckling to the king and unduly deferring to his belief in witchcraft, as untrue to the Hebrew text, and as relying too much on the Greek Septuagint. The personal integrity of the translators was impugned. Among other things, they were accused of "blasphemy," "most damnable corruptions," "intolerable deceit," and "vile imposture," the critic who used these epithets being careful to say that they were not "the dictates of passion but the just resentment of a zealous mind." In due time, it prevailed, however; and for more than two and a half centuries, no other authorized translation of the Bible into English was made. The King James Version became the "Authorized Version" of the English-speaking people.

In the 1850s, a movement toward revision of the Authorized Version began to gather strength, and in 1870, the Convocation of the Province of Canterbury appointed a Committee to undertake it. The Revised Version of the New Testament was published in 1881 and the Revised Version of the Old Testament in 1885. The American Standard Version, a variant edition containing the renderings preferred by the American scholars who had cooperated in the work of revision, was published in 1901. The revised versions of 1881-1901 made permanent advances in two respects: their recognition of the principle that Hebrew poetry is to be translated as poetry, in characteristic parallelism, and their affording due weight to the text of the ancient Greek manuscripts of the New Testament that had been discovered since 1611.

The English Revised Version and the American Standard Version are far more faithful and accurate translations of the Word of God, as found in the Greek New Testament, than the King James Version. But with all their accuracy, the revised versions of 1881 and 1901 lost some of the beauty and power of the King James Version. This is because they are too obviously "translation English." They are mechanically exact, literal, word-for-word translations that follow the order of the Greek words, as far as this is possible, rather than the order that is natural to English.

The copyright of the American Standard Version was given in 1929 to the International Council of Religious Education, which appointed a committee of fifteen Biblical scholars to have charge of the text. For more than two years, the Committee wrestled with the problem of whether or not a revision of the American Standard Version should be undertaken; and if so, what should be the nature and extent of the revision. Finally, the Committee decided that there should be a thorough revision of the Version of 1901, which would stay as close to the Tyndale-King James tradition as it could in the light of our present knowledge of the Greek text and its meaning on the one hand and our present understanding of English on the other. This decision having been reached, the work of the Committee was suspended because of lack of funds. In 1936, a contract was negotiated with Thomas Nelson and Sons, publishers of the American Standard Version, to finance the work of revision by advance royalties, in return for which they were afforded the exclusive right to publish the Revised Standard Version for a period of ten years. Thereafter, it was to be open to other publishers under specified conditions.

There were four major reasons for undertaking the revision of the King James Version:

1. The King James Version was based upon a few late medieval manuscripts, and these, especially in the New Testament, contained the accumulated errors of many centuries of manuscript copying.

2. The previous seventy-five years had been an age of discoveries in the archaeology of the Near East and had afforded to scholars new knowledge of the history, geography, and cultures of Biblical lands and rich new resources for understanding the vocabulary, grammar, and idioms of the Biblical languages.

3. The seventeenth-century English of the King James Version is increasingly a barrier between it and the reader. The greatest problem is presented by the hundreds of English words that are still in constant use but now convey a different meaning from that which they had in the King James Version. These words were accurate translations of the Hebrew and Greek Scriptures in 1611 but had become misleading.

4. The general excellence of the King James Version as "the noblest monument of English prose" must not blind us to the fact that it contains a substantial number of errors in translation, some infelicities in expression, and some renderings that are ambiguous or obscure.

Let me make these statements concrete by citing a few examples under each.

1. The Greek text used by the King James translators of the New Testament was that edited by Beza, 1589, who closely followed the text published by Erasmus, 1516-35, which had been based upon only eight manuscripts, the oldest of which was from the tenth century. We now possess about 4500 Greek manuscripts of the Scriptures, of which about two hundred are really ancient, written in uncial (capital) letters; and we are far better equipped to recover what was the original wording of the Greek text. The best of these manuscripts are from the third, fourth, and fifth centuries. The evidence for the text of the books of the New Testament is better than for any other ancient book, both in the number of extant manuscripts and in the nearness of the date of some of these manuscripts to the date when the book was originally written. For the text of Homer, there are a few more than one hundred manuscripts, the best of which were written in the tenth or eleventh century A.D. Our knowledge of the text of Plato depends upon less than two hundred manuscripts, and the best of these are from the ninth and tenth centuries A.D.

The errors in the Erasmus-Beza text, and hence in the King James Version, are of all sorts—omissions, substitutions, additions, and in some cases deliberate changes made by a copyist who thought the manuscripts before him needed correction.

In Acts 4:25, the Greek text used by the King James translators had lost the words "by the Holy Spirit"; in Acts 16:7, Paul's guidance on his way to take the gospel to Europe is attributed to "the Spirit" instead of "the Spirit of Jesus," as the most ancient manuscripts have it; in 1 Peter 2:2, the apostle's exhortation to "grow up to salvation" was reduced by copyists to the simple injunction to "grow." The original text in James 4:12 read, "There is one lawgiver and judge, he who is able to save and to destroy. But who are you that you judge your neighbor?" Beginning with the eighth century, manuscripts lost the words "and judge," and thereby lost the point of the passage.

In Romans 8:28, the King James Version reads: "We know that all things work together for good to them that love God." The present version has "We know that in everything God works for good with those who love him." The subject of the sentence is "God" in two of the oldest and best manuscripts, Vaticanus and Alexandrinus; in some ancient versions; and in some passages in Origen. But this had dropped out of the vast majority of manuscripts and did not appear in the Greek text that the King James translators used. The discovery of the Chester Beatty Papyri has now brought powerful support to this as the ancient reading. These papyri are the earliest known manuscripts of Paul's letter, probably a century older than Vaticanus; and the Chester Beatty manuscript of Romans 8:28 has "God" as the subject of the sentence. With this weighty new evidence, the Committee for the Revised Standard Version no longer hesitated to translate the verse: "We know that in everything God works for good with those who love him."

A copyist's error in writing *epioei* for *eporei* (Mark 6:20) caused the King James Version to say that Herod "did many things" when he heard John the Baptist, while the most ancient manuscripts say that he "was much perplexed." A misreading of the Greek letters changed the description of the beast in Revelation 17:8, "it was and is not and is to come" (*Kai parestai*) to the mystifying contradiction of the King James rendering, "that was, and is not, and yet is" (*kaiper esti*).

A typical example of intended improvement is in Ephesians 5:30, "we are members of his body." The sentence ends with that statement in the Codex Sinaiticus, the Codex Vaticanus, and the Codex Alexandrinus, the three great uncial manuscripts that, because of their age and their relative completeness, have stood together in the first rank of our resources for the text of the New Testament. The Sinaiticus and the Vaticanus were written in the fourth century and the Alexandrinus in the fifth century. The Sinaiticus, however, contains at this point a marginal addition written in by someone in the seventh century. He inserted after the original statement, "we are members of his body," the words "from his flesh and from his bones." The Greek text used by the King James translators contained the addition, and they did the best they could with it by treating the inserted words as though they stood in apposition with "of his body," despite the fact that the Greek construction is quite different. They translated the verse: "For we are members of his body, of his flesh, and of his bones."

The copyist who added the expression "openly" to the promise in the Sermon on the Mount, "your Father who sees in secret will reward you" (Matthew 6:4, 6, 18), probably did not realize that he was blurring over, if not contradicting, the whole point of our Lord's teaching in these verses. Where Paul counsels husband and wife to give to each other what is "due" (1 Corinthians 7:2), copyists added the word for "good will," and the King James Version flattened it out to read: "Let the husband render unto the wife due benevolence; and likewise also the wife unto the husband."

For the Old Testament, only late manuscripts survive (except for the recently discovered Dead Sea texts of Isaiah and Habakkuk and some fragments of other books), and these contain the Hebrew text as standardized by Jewish scholars (the Masoretes) of the sixth to ninth centuries. This text contains some errors that had accumulated in the centuries of manuscript copying before the Masoretes did their work. The best way to discover and correct these earlier errors is to turn to the ancient versions of the books of the Old Testament (translations into Greek, Aramic, Syriac, and Latin) that were made before the time of the Masoretic standardization and therefore reflect earlier forms of the text.

For example, in 1 Samuel 14:41 is recorded Saul's appeal to the Lord to disclose whose sin was responsible for His displeasure. It reads in the Revised Standard Version: "O Lord God of Israel, why hast thou not answered thy servant this day? If this guilt is in me or in Jonathan my son, O LORD God of Israel, give Urim; but if this guilt is in thy people Israel, give Thummim." By a copyist's error, all of this prayer that lies between the first and last occurrences of the word "Israel" has been lost from the Hebrew text, which would be literally translated, "Saul said to the LORD God of Israel, Give Thummim." The infelicity of representing Saul as dictating to God was avoided by use of the vowels for tamim, which means "perfect," and the King James translators rendered the text, "Give a perfect *lot*." The revisers in the 1870s, dissatisfied with this, rendered it yet more freely, "Show the right." Yet all the while the wording of the prayer had been preserved in the Greek and Latin versions; and it now appears in the Revised Standard Version, with a marginal note indicating its source.

2. The second major reason for undertaking revision of our English translation of the Bible was the wealth of new knowledge resulting from the archaeological discoveries of the preceding seventy-five years. An amazing body of Greek papyri has been brought to bear upon the study of New Testament Greek and has shown that it is like the spoken vernacular of the first century A.D. and is not the classical Greek that the King James translators in 1611 and the revisers in the 1870s supposed it to be. A vast quantity of writings in related Semitic languages, some of them only recently discovered, has greatly enlarged our knowledge of the vocabulary and grammar of Biblical Hebrew and Aramaic.

An example of better understanding of Biblical history is the present translation of 1 Kings 10:28. This passage is concerned with King Solomon's importation of great numbers of horses with which he equipped his chariots and his cavalry. Verse 28 contains two occurrences of a Hebrew word that has puzzled translators. The word is *miqweh*. The King James Version translates the verse: "And Solomon had horses brought out of Egypt, and linen yarn: the king's merchants received the linen yarn at a price." The revisers of the 1870s felt sure that linen yarn had nothing to do with these horses, and so they made a brave conjecture and translated the verse: "And the horses which Solomon had were brought out of Egypt; and the king's merchants received them in droves, each drove at a price." But Assyrian records uncovered by archaeology have shown that this word must contain a reference to a place named Kue, in Asia Minor, later known as Cilicia. The verse is now translated: "And Solomon's import of horses was from Egypt and Kue, and the king's traders received them from Kue at a price." This rendering is supported by the Vulgate and indirectly by the Septuagint. Solomon's commerce in horses has been verified strikingly by the discovery at Megiddo of complete stable compounds at which horses were kept.

3. The reader of the King James Version of the Bible, who is not acquainted with the Hebrew and Greek, often fails to get the meaning of a Scriptural passage because it is couched in the English of 1611. There are more than three hundred English words in this version which at that time were accurate translations of the Hebrew and Greek but which now have so changed in meaning that they have become misleading. They no longer say to the reader what the King James translators meant them to say.

When the Psalmist says (119, 147) "I prevented the dawning of the morning," the present-day reader of the King James Version is mystified. He may then consult the Revised Version of 1901, where he or she will read, "I anticipated the dawning of the morning"–by which the reader will probably understand that the writer eagerly looked forward to the dawn. The Revised Standard Version expresses the meaning of the Hebrew clearly, "I rise before dawn." This is a part of the description of the devotional habits of a pious Jew who rises before the dawn to begin the day with meditation and prayer.

In the King James Version of Isaiah 43:14, God speaks through the prophet: "There is none that can deliver out of my hand: I will work, and who shall let it?" But the meaning is "who can hinder it?" "Suffer little children to come to me" means "Let the children come to me." The word "conversation" in the King James Version means "conduct," "behavior," or "manner of life." The verb "communicate" has the sense of "share." It refers, not to words, but to fellowship and generous action. When the author of the letter to the Hebrews writes (13:16) "to do good and to communicate forget not," he is not urging them to gossip or to companionable speech or to regular communion in the Lord's Supper but to the sharing of their worldly goods. The Revised Standard Version translation is, "do not neglect to do good and to share what you have."

To "allege" now means merely to assert, but in the sixteenth century, it meant to adduce evidence, hence to cite or quote authorities. That is what it means in Acts 17:3, where we are told by the King James Version that for three weeks Paul "reasoned with them out of the scriptures, opening and alleging that Christ must needs have suffered and risen again from the dead." The Revised Standard Version translates the passage: "They came to Thessalonica, where there was a synagogue of the Jews. And Paul went in, as was his custom, and for three weeks he argued with them from the scriptures, explaining and proving that it was necessary for the Christ to suffer and to rise from the dead, and saying, 'This Jesus, whom I proclaim to you, is the Christ.' "

"Take no thought for the morrow" means "Do not be anxious about tomorrow" (Matthew 6:34). "Take no thought how or what ye shall speake" means "Do not be anxious how you are to speak or what you are to say" (Matthew 10:19). "Be careful for nothing" means "Have no anxiety about anything" (Philippians 4:6). "I would have you without carefulness" means "I want you to be free from all anxieties" (1 Corinthians 7:32). When Jesus gently reproved Martha for being "careful about many things," it was for being "anxious" (Luke 10:40). In all these cases, we are dealing with the Greek word for anxiety; the English words "thought," "carefulness," and "careful" were sound enough translations of it in the sixteenth century, but today they gravely mislead the English reader.

"Immediately" and "straightway" are two words much used in the New Testament, which leave no doubt as to their meaning. But unfortunately, the Greek words that mean immediately and straightway have also been translated in the King James Version by the terms "anon," "by and by," and "presently," all of which once meant immediately and now mean soon or after a while. When Jesus entered Peter's house in Capernaum, they told him immediately that Peter's mother-in-law was ill; but the King James Version (Mark 1:30) gives the modern reader the impression that they did a bit of visiting first, for it says that "anon" they told him of her. Salome demanded that the head of John the Baptist be given her on a platter immediately (Mark 6:25), but the King James Version says that she asked that it be given her "by and by."

"Wealth." is used in the sense of weal or well-being. Unless we remember this, the King James rendering of 1 Corinthians 10:24 looks like encouragement to theft: "Let no man seek his own, but every man another's wealth." The word "virtue" has nothing to do with moral character in the statement made by Jesus when a woman touched Him in the hope of being healed: "Somebody hath touched me, for I perceive that virtue is gone out of me." "Virtue" here means nothing more than "power," and "power" is the only proper translation of the Greek term that is used, *dynamis* (Luke 8:46).

It is confusing for young people today, who are being told that respect for persons is a basic principle of sound democracy and true religion, to read in the Bible that "God is no respecter of persons" (Acts 10:34) and to find that same idea repeated in one form or another in a dozen passages in the New Testament. The Greek word *prosopolemptes*, which is translated "respecter of persons," means "acceptor of the face," and the Latin equivalent is *acceptor personae*, that is, acceptor of the mask that an actor wore. When the King James Bible was published, the English word "person" was still close to this primary meaning of the Latin word *persona*, mask. It referred to the outward appearance of individuals' circumstances–wealth, birth, power–rather than to intrinsic worth or to the inner springs of conscious, self-determining being. This text and others using similar words mean simply that God does not regard mere externals. The expression was kept in the revised version of 1881 and 1901 but is given up in all other modern translations. Moffatt's translation is "God has no favorites"; and Goodspeed's "God shows no partiality." The Revised Standard Version follows Goodspeed here, and both are in fact returning to William Tyndale, whose translation was "God is not partial."

4. The fourth reason for revision of the English Bible is the need to correct the mistranslations and to clear up the obscurities, ambiguities and infelicities of expression that at various points mar the general excellence of the King James Version.

This version represents Jesus as saying, when He offered the cup to His disciples at the Last Supper, "Drink ye all of it." But in the Greek of which this is supposed to be a translation, the word for "all" is in the nominative case. It modifies the subject of the verb, not its object. Jesus did not tell His disciples to drink all of the contents of the cup; He invited all of them to drink. This was correctly expressed in some of the earlier English translations. Tyndale had: "Drink of it every one." The Geneva Bible had: "Drink ye every one of it." The present Revised Standard Version reads: "Drink of it, all of you."

In James 3:2, the King James Version reads: "For in many things we offend all." That seems to mean that we are offensive to everybody. But here again the Greek word for "all" is in the nominative case; it is not the object of the verb but modifies the subject. And here again, the earlier English translations had been correct. The King James translators fell into ambiguity by copying the rendering of the Catholic Rhemish Version. The American Standard Version of 1901 reads: "for in many things we all stumble." The Revised Standard Version reads: "for we all make many mistakes."

In John 10:16, the King James Version reads, "And other sheep I have, which are not of this fold: them also I must bring, and they shall hear my voice; and there shall be one fold, and one shepherd." The Greek word for "fold" that is used in the first part of this verse is different from the word used toward the end, which means "flock." Jesus did not say that all of His followers will be in one fold but that they all belong to His one flock. This verse was correctly translated by Tyndale, but King James accepted the error from the Bishops' Bible.

The chief priests did not "covenant with" Judas for thirty pieces of silver (Matthew 26:15); they "paid him thirty pieces of silver."

"He that giveth, let him do it with simplicity" (Romans 12:8) is an oddly misleading exhortation in view of the fact that the word here represented by "simplicity" means, and is so translated in similar contexts of the King James Version, "liberality."

Paul's injunction to the Thessalonians is not "Abstain from all appearance of evil," as King James puts it, but "Abstain from every form of evil" (1 Thessalonians 5:22). King James causes Paul to make a strange claim of sinlessness in 2 Corinthians 5:21: "For he hath made him to be sin for us, who knew no sin." But Paul said nothing that can be translated "for us, who knew no sin." The Revised Standard Version has: "For our sake he made him to be sin who knew no sin."

Paul is represented as writing to the Romans (6:17): "God be thanked, that ye were the servants of sin, but ye have obeyed." The present translation is "Thanks be to God, that you who once were slaves of sin have become obedient."

"In your patiences possess ye your souls" (Luke 21:19) is correctly translated, "By your endurance you will gain your lives." The Pharisee's statement, "I give tithes of all that I possess" (Luke 18:12) is properly "I give tithes of all that I get"–that is, the tithe is based upon income rather than upon capital. Paul's counsel to the Thessalonians that each should "know how to possess his vessel" (1 Thessalonians 4:4) means "know how to take a wife." Paul did not insult the Athenians by calling them "too superstitious" (Acts 17:22); he won a sympathetic hearing by saying, "I perceive that in every way you are very religious."

By a printer's error, the original edition of the King James Version (Matthew 23:24) had "strain at a gnat" instead of "strain out a gnat"; and by some odd perversity of human nature this error remains in the text of the King James Version today, and some persons will even argue that it is a correct translation. But the Greek means "strain out," and that is what all the earlier English versions had, from Tyndale to the Bishops' Bible. The King James Version stands alone in this error.

Another printer's change is in 1 Timothy 2:9, where the King James translators wrote: "That women adorn themselves in modest apparel, with shamefastness and sobriety." The text thus appeared in 1611 and for sixty years thereafter. Then, through some printer's error, the word "shamefacedness" appeared, and it has been kept to this day. That is entirely unfair to the translators, for the word that they used, "shamefastness," referred to character while "shamefacedness" refers to appearance. Paul may be accused of failing to afford to women their full and proper place, but at least he did not exhort them to go about shamefacedly. The Revised Standard Version translates this text: "that women should adorn themselves modestly and sensibly in seemly apparel."

It chanced that I was in England in the summer following the publication of the Revised Standard Version of the New Testament, and I was asked by an old friend, an English minister, to show him a copy. He read in it here and there and expressed his interest in various passages; then turned to the thirteenth chapter of 1 Corinthians, which he read slowly. He handed the book back to me with the comment: "It's very good, but I still like 'charity.' I think I'll keep on with the Authorised Version, where I can say 'charity.' It is such a beautiful word."

I controlled my impulse to tell him what I thought of a decision based on such trivial and irrelevant grounds, and we still remain friends.

But surely the important thing is not what he would like to have in the Bible but what is there; no matter how beautiful a word is, our question must always be, is it true? And "charity" is not the true word in that chapter in which he loved to repeat it so unctuously.

The noun *agape* and its correlative verb and adjective appear in the Greek New Testament three hundred and twelve times. It was correctly translated as "love" by Tyndale and all other sixteenth-century versions up to the Bishops' Bible. In the second edition of the latter, it was translated as "charity" in thirty-two cases and the King James Bible used "charity" in twenty-six of these.

The distribution of these twenty-six cases is peculiar. None appears before 1 Corinthians 8:1. Eleven of the twenty-six are in 1 Corinthians, and eight of these in chapter 13. There is no good reason, no principle of literature or logic or ethics or theology to explain why the word "charity" should be used in these twenty-six cases, while the word "love" is used in the other two hundred and eighty-six cases.

The second edition of the Bishops' Bible and the King James Bible stand alone in this strange substitution of "charity" for "love" in less than 10 percent of the cases of the occurrence of *agape* and its correlatives. The revised versions of 1881 and 1901 returned to the practice of the earlier sixteenth-century versions and used "love" throughout; and they have been followed in this by all modern translations based upon the original Greek.

By so doing, the modern translations give a surer undergirding to the basic Christian doctrine of God and humanity than does the King James Version. The basic principle and ultimate motive of both the Christian gospel and the Christian ethic is love. God is love, and we love because He first loved us. In the translation of the Greek word for *agape*, we are dealing not with a mere exhortation to feeling and action, or even with a statement of human duty, but with the ultimate grounding of human duty and destiny in the very nature and eternal purpose of God. Whatever would tend to separate human love from divine love or to weaken the essential connection between the Christian ethic and the Christian gospel is wrong. Yet that is just what the King James Version does in those twenty-six cases that it tears out of the total fabric of the New Testament teaching.

The eighty years since 1870 have been marked by interest and activity in the English translation of the Bible that are without parallel except in the eighty-five years between the publication of Tyndale's first translation in 1525 and the publication of the King James Version in 1611.

In the sixteenth century, the problem was to bring the Bible directly to the English people in their own tongue and to secure a translation from the original Hebrew and Greek that would emancipate them from the thousand-year dependence of the church upon the Latin Vulgate. It took repeated efforts at translation before the King James finally won its way to general use. The effect of these translations was tremendous. Green says in his *Short History of the English People*: "England became the people of a book, and that book was the Bible. . . . Everywhere its words kindled a startling enthusiasm. . . . Greater than its effect on literature or social life was the effect of the Bible on the character of the people. . . . The whole temper of the nation felt the change. A new conception of life and of man superseded the old." In the seventeenth century, this new conception of life and of humanity challenged the absolutism of the Stuart kings and led to the enactment of the Bill of Rights in 1689. In the eighteenth century, the principles set forth in the Bill of Rights were thought through and lived out on American soil, and they eventuated in our Declaration of Independence. The English-speaking peoples owe to William Tyndale, to the Geneva Bible, and to the King James Bible an incalculable debt.

The problem today is to bring the Bible to people in a translation that they can understand and to emancipate them from a blind adherence to the King James Version that gravely impairs our understanding and limits the impact of the Bible upon our lives.

The present Committee has not sought to make a translation of the Bible that will be as up-to-date in its phrasing as is possible or even one that is consistently and consciously up-to-date. Such a translation would inevitably be ephemeral. There is truth, moreover, in Archbishop Trench's statement that "it is good that the phraseology of Scripture should not be exactly that of our common life; that it should be removed from the vulgarities, and even the familiarities, of this; just as there is a sense of fitness which dictates that the architecture of a church should be different from that of a house."

The Committee has sought to express the meaning of the Bible in simple, enduring words that are worthy to stand in the great tradition of Tyndale and the King James Version, purged of its archaisms and made clear in meaning. They tried to use relatively timeless words and idioms instead of those that are merely the language of our time. And they have kept to the basic structure of the tradition, conscious that their work is that of revisers and seeking to maintain its disciplined freedom and compactness. I do believe, however, that it is better than any other English version. At no period in history have people needed the great truths of the Bible more than we need them now. It is a good providence that has led Protestants, Catholics, and Jews alike to renewed study of the Scriptures and to the preparation of revisions of the older translations in the light of what we now know concerning the ancient text and its meaning. And it is good that in Great Britain, Holland, France, Germany, and so on around the world, similar work is in progress. May it all further our understanding of the Scriptures and help to deepen our faith in God.

6

IMAGINATION AND OBJECTIVITY OF MIND

"Then said Abishai to David, God hath delivered up thine enemy into thy hand this day; now therefore let me smite him, I pray thee, with the spear to the earth at one stroke, and I will not smite him the second time. And David said to Abishai, Destroy him not: for who can put forth his hand against the Lord's anointed, and be guiltless?

I Samuel 26:8, 9

Mr. Elmer Davis, in his stirring novel entitled *Giant-Killer*, has torn away the halo of sanctity with which tradition has crowned David. I think that Mr. Davis has carried the debunking process so far as to be a bit unfair, but at least he has reminded us that David was in fact a rough, passionate, red-bearded soldier of fortune. He was a crafty strategist who won by deceit as often as by force. He had an uncanny knack of turning to advantage the mistakes and foibles of others and, like a cat, adroitly falling on his feet. He could, on occasion, be as unscrupulous as Metternich and Napoleon.

He was a born leader. He had a way with women that made them readily compliant with his desires. He had a way with men that bound them to him in loyalty so reckless that they would risk their lives at the suggestion even of his whim.

David was an outlaw, fleeing for his life from the malice of King Saul. He sought refuge in a cave in the wilderness. Hither came to him, says the ancient chronicler, "everyone that was in distress, and every-

Text for this chapter was originally the commencement address at Gettysburg College in 1934. It was published in the volume of collected sermons by Luther Weigle, *We Are Able*, in 1937 and is used here by permission of Harper and Row, Publishers.

one that was in debt, and everyone that was discontented"; and he was what in these days we would call a racketeer, for he and his followers exacted tribute from wealthy owners of lands and flocks as payment for a "protection" that they did not ask or want.

I

Yet on one occasion, David resisted a great temptation. Saul brought an army of three thousand men into the wilderness, determined to find David and put him to death. With characteristic daring, David decided to visit Saul's camp at night, taking with him but one of his followers. By a lapse of military discipline so strange and exceptional that the chronicler accounts it a miracle they found all of Saul's army asleep.

David and Abishai stealthily penetrate to the inner circle of wagons, drawn up in barricade to protect the king. There they find Saul. And he too lies in a sleep so deep that it is like the spell of a magician or a miracle of God. It is the chance of a lifetime, thinks Abishai. He whispers quickly to David–a whisper that begins like the lilt of a flute and ends up like the hiss of a serpent: "God hath delivered up thine enemy into thy hand this day; now therefore let me smite him, I pray thee, with the spear to the earth at one stroke, and I will not smite him the second time."

It was a tremendous temptation. Most men in David's place would have yielded to it. But not he. To Abishai's amazement, he shakes his head in refusal. "Destroy him not: for who can put forth his hand against the Lord's anointed, and be guiltless?"

That is a dramatic, unexpected turn to this adventure. If we know anything about David, we are as surprised as Abishai. His decision confronts us with a problem in human psychology. What caused David, who did not hesitate at deliberate, cold-blooded murder in furtherance of his ends, to reject so perfect an opportunity to destroy his foe? What inhibited within him the powerful drives of self-preservation, revenge, ambition that reinforced Abishai's suggestion.

The answer lies, I think, in the name by which David refers to Saul. It is different from that which Abishai used. Abishai called him "thine enemy"; David calls him "the Lord's anointed."

Abishai had a single-track mind. He thought of but one thing–that here was the body of Saul, who could be slain by a single stroke of the spear. But David saw more. He saw not only Saul but the prophet Samuel, the tribes of Israel, the emerging kingdom so essential to the welfare of his people, the will and purpose of God. David had imagination. From the standpoint of the psychology of human motives, we have in this old story a case of impulse checked by imagination, imagination disciplined by purpose, and purpose conceived in objectivity of mind.

II

David's forbearance was due to the fact that he stopped to think. He had not been trained by the slogans of modern advertising to "obey that impulse" or taught by popular psychology the evil inward effects of repressing an instinct. He was an unsophisticated human being who stopped to think, who let his impulse be checked by imagination.

Just what he thought we do not know. But we can make a fairly good guess. In imagination, there passed before his mind's eye, in swift dramatic rehearsal, the probable outcomes of such a deed. In imagination, he foresaw what men would think and say and do; and from what he thus foresaw he turned away.

David's concern was for the kingdom. The cause for which he lived and strove was that a stable government of his people might be established and endure and that they might win and hold their place under the sun. The tribes of Israel had found it hard to give up their nomad ways, and for more than a century after the death of Joshua, their quarrels with one another made them easy prey for the better-organized nations around them. "In those days there was no king in Israel: every man did that which was right in his own eyes," mourns the chronicler at the close of each wild tale of bloody adventure and defeat. Finally, acting in the name of God, the prophet Samuel had chosen Saul and had anointed him king. Under Saul's faults, he was the king, the Lord's anointed, the symbol and center of the hopes of the Hebrew people. To assassinate him in the interest of personal revenge would be disastrous to the kingdom. It would start a feud. Israel would split again into warring camps and be at the mercy of its enemies. That David must not, will not do. His decision is made. Imagination conquers impulse.

III

Yet the victory is not to imagination alone. The power lies in imagination disciplined and steadied by purpose. Without purpose, imagination may becloud the issue. It may actually become an instrument of self-deception, covering actual motives with a gilding of respectability and rationalization that hide their real character.

How easily David could have rationalized the deed to which Abishai tempted him! It would be simple, elemental justice, for one thing. Saul had persistently, murderously sought David, hating him without reason, and this would be but retribution. It could be construed as self-defense, for David would never be free from jeopardy and fear while this implacable enemy remained. It would be in the best interest of the kingdom, for Saul had a touch of madness, and his malady grew worse with the passing years. It would be in line with the purposes of God, for God had promised, through the prophet Samuel, that David should be king; and the deep sleep into which Saul and his army had fallen might well be a miracle of divine providence. Moreover, the instrument of providence was at hand; Abishai would deal the fatal stroke. David needed only to remain silent or to turn away; it was not necessary for him even to nod assent or to utter the Hebrew equivalents of the potent letters "O.K."

I confess that I am surprised and a bit abashed at the ease with which I can find plausible reasons for David to kill Saul. Perhaps we sophisticated moderns are too ready and facile with our rationalizations.

IV

But David wasted no time dallying with considerations such as these. His decision reflects steadiness of purpose and remarkable objectivity of mind. Objectivity is a rare and difficult virtue. It is not easy to pass over one's personal likes and dislikes, to ignore old grudges, to avoid deflection of judgment by self-interest, to escape wishful thinking, to consider the situation objectively and on its merits, and so to reach valid conclusions. It is not easy when A whispers that B is thine enemy and when you know that B is your enemy to remember that B is the Lord's anointed and to treat him as such.

Yet such objectivity of mind is absolutely essential if you would be capable of any great enterprise that depends upon human cooperation. History has no finer examples, perhaps, than the man whose destiny it was to bear the burden of our own Civil War and to save the Union—Abraham Lincoln. The three men of Lincoln's Cabinet who did most to help him sustain that burden and win through to victory—Seward, Chase, and Stanton—had treated him with contempt and even insult. Soon after Lincoln's inauguration, Seward wrote him an amazing letter, expressing in thinly veiled terms his feeling that Lincoln was incompetent to deal with the great issues confronting the country and offering himself to assume the responsibility of national leadership. Lincoln gently but firmly showed him that that could not be, and they worked together in loyal friendship to the end. While yet a member of the Cabinet, Chase sought to be nominated for the presidency in Lincoln's place; but Lincoln cherished no resentment and soon thereafter appointed him Chief Justice of the Supreme Court of the United States. Stanton openly insulted Lincoln when they first met at a court of law in Illinois, refused to continue with a case if Lincoln were to be associated with him, and profanely called him a "gawky, long-armed ape."

But in time, Lincoln said, "The War Department has demonstrated the great necessity for a Secretary of Mr. Stanton's great ability, and I have made up my mind to sit down on all my pride–it may be a portion of my self-respect–and appoint him to the place." His trust was justified, and in the end, it was Stanton who stood by Lincoln's deathbed and in reverent awe pronounced the solemn verdict: "Now he belongs to the ages."

V

When I conceived this sermon, it was my thought to seek an example of failure to maintain such objectivity of mind. I have decided not to name any such. Read any of the books that deal with the events of the past twenty years–histories, biographies, letters, records of diplomacy. Read Mark Sullivan's fifth volume of *Our Times*, entitled *Over Here*. Read Theodor Wolff's poignant account of European diplomacy, *The Eve of 1914.* See how inextricably personal factors are involved in the chain of events that led to, and have issued from, the World War of 1914-18; see how statesmen have harbored grudges, and the fates of nations have hung upon personal issues that were in themselves trivial.

There are always two ways that one can follow. We can yield to impulse or order our lives by intelligence. We can deceive ourselves by rationalizing the drift of desire or control our action by the exercise of reasonable choice among alternatives and their foreseen consequences. We can let our minds dwell upon the meanness, pettiness, and evil of our fellows or we can seek to engage them and ourselves in purposes that lift us above our quarrels and give dignity and worth to life.

No one can doubt which of these ways befits the educated man. It is the way of imagination, of reason, of objective-mindedness, of faith in the possibilities of human nature.

The most ominous portent of our time is that we have so largely lost faith in one another. We distrust human nature. Human nature will not change, is the cry of both the stand-pat conservative and the impatient, violent radical. At bottom, both hold, human nature is just physical hunger, animal lust, and brute selfishness. Imagination, reason, goodwill, and objectivity of mind may have their day when no great issue is at stake, but when life itself is threatened, we revert to the primitive drives. Man may be moral in his immediate, face-to-face relationships, it is asserted; but society in its larger, impersonal groupings, class-to-class and nation-to-nation, is immoral, knowing no final law save the victory of force.

"Human history becomes more and more a race between education and catastrophe," wrote H.G. Wells after World War I. The years that have followed have deepened the somber truth and sharpened the challenge of that sentence. If the world is to avoid catastrophe, it will be because education succeeds in equipping men to cope with the intricate and desperate problems that confront them today. It will be because schools and colleges send forth a generation of young men and women with imaginations sensitive and resourceful; with purposes generously conceived and loyally pursued; with ability to face facts honestly, seeking only the truth; and with that objectivity of mind that subordinates personal advantage to the common welfare.

Much in our time inclines men to cynicism and despair; there are even forebodings that civilization is doomed. But that need not be. No fate is driving us to ruin. We have no cosmic enemy. Our failures are our own. We can turn, if we will, to the higher way. It is still possible, as Paul put it, to be transformed by the renewing of our minds that we may prove the good and acceptable and perfect will of God.

7

THE COURAGE TO BE LIBERAL

So faith, hope, love abide; these three; but the greatest of these is love.

1 Corinthians 13:13

I want to speak to you on the Courage to Be Liberal. It takes courage to be liberal in these days, and it is not always clear just what path of action to follow. Yet the spirit of the liberal is unmistakable. It is the spirit described by Paul in this matchless chapter.

Paul was writing to a lot of sham liberals—people who felt emancipated both from the scruples of the Jewish law and from the superstitions of pagan mythology. They were contentious, self-centered, and self-indulgent. To be liberal, they thought, is to decry the scruples of others and to have no scruples of one's own.

Such is not the liberty of the Christian gospel, says Paul; they are merely showing lack of self-control. This letter is one of the sharpest that he ever wrote. The true liberals, he asserts, who are experiencing the real freedom that is in Christ Jesus, are those in whom liberty is disciplined by love.

That Paul was himself a liberal, I do not pause to debate. If by a liberal, we mean one devoted to liberty, one who loves his fellowmen, and, best of all, one who actually frees his fellows and posterity from some crippling restraint or limitation, then surely Paul was liberal—Paul, who under God freed the Christian message from bondage to legalism and started it on its way to men of every race; Paul, who found the Christian gospel confined to an incipient Jewish sect and expanded it

This address was given during the centennial celebration of The Packer Collegiate Institute. It was then published in *Education and the Faith of America*: Addresses Given During the Centennial Celebration of the Packer Collegiate Institute, in 1945.

to a worldwide mission; Paul, for whom there was neither Jew nor Greek, barbarian, Scythian, slave, or freeman, but for whom all are members of the human family, meant to be sons and heirs of God. In any roster of the great liberals of human history, Paul must stand close to Jesus, who was the greatest liberal of them all.

I am using the word "liberal," obviously, to denote a certain quality of the human spirit rather than as the label of a party. When William E. Channing, in 1819, preached the sermon that became a platform for the Unitarian movement in this country, he was urged to adopt the name "Liberal." But he refused, saying that it seemed to him presumptuous to use that word as the designation of a party because it may be applied to men in many fields and with a wide variety of opinions. His modesty might well be emulated. The spirit of the liberal is too great, too far-reaching, too vital to be preempted by any one party, whether in politics or in theology.

The fact is that parties come and go, but the spirit of the liberal abides. The struggle for human freedom is waged always at those points where freedom is threatened by power or abridged by privilege or confined by tradition. These points change. The lines of battle shift. It may even happen that the protagonists of liberty later become its opponents, when in their hands some hard-won victory for freedom lapses into privilege and new conditions propound new duties.

There is no reason to be dismayed, therefore, when you learn that at some point or other the position of a liberal party or school has been transcended. The great English liberals of the eighteenth and nineteenth centuries, from Adam Smith to Bentham and Mill and Spencer, believed not only in the perfectibility of the human race but in unrestricted competition and *laissez-faire* as the instruments of inevitable human progress. We now see that they were, to say the least, partly mistaken. For nineteenth-century liberals in Biblical scholarship, such as Adolph Harnack, the essence of Christianity was a simple and genial affair, based upon what they called the gospel of Jesus, as recorded in his sayings in the synoptic gospels; but it now appears that their picture of Jesus was too sketchy and that the gospel about Jesus cannot be ignored. Nineteenth-century liberals in theology revolted from that utter pessimism with respect to human nature into which Calvinistic orthodoxy had fallen, and their revolt was emancipating; but the humanism that issued from it went so far as to forget that there is such a thing as sin and to think of God as a mere appendage to man's desires. From such humanism, we are now rightly experiencing a decided reaction. When you read, then, as you probably will, of "the disintegration of liberalism" or "the decline of liberal theology"—I do not say when you hear these phrases, for I doubt whether the faculty of this college has much use for them--it will be well for you to remember that they refer for the most part to these three things: the loss of confidence in the inevitability of human progress, the abandonment of a too simple interpretation of the gospels, and the failure of humanism.

But the spirit of the liberal goes on. To use Paul's phrases, our prophecies pass away, our tongues our curious watchwords, emotional slogans, and party cries--cease, the knowledge of each generation is superseded in the next, but faith, hope, and love abide. And these are the spirit of the liberal.

But what does Paul mean by love? At the risk of seeming pedantic, I remind you that three quite different Greek words are translated into English by the one word "love." *Eros* means sexual love, lust, and passion; *philia* means affection and friendship; *agape* means respect and goodwill. *Eros* and *philia* refer to feelings and emotions; they involve personal intimacy. *Agape*, on the contrary, is an attitude of will and choice; it does not necessarily involve intimacy. The characteristic word that is translated "love" in the New Testament is *agape*. With its corresponding verb, it is used more than two hundred and fifty times, whereas *philia* and its verb appear only twenty-five times. *Eros* is not used at all. When we are told that God is love and that the two great commandments are to love God and to love our fellowmen, the word is *agape* or its verb. The love of God for man, of man for God, and of man for man, which is enjoined in the New Testament, is not a matter of the emotions or of spontaneous personal affections. It lies within the realm of will and choice.

Christian love is no weakly sentimental thing. It is robust and realistic. It is based upon the ethical principle of respect for personality. "Thou shalt love thy neighbor as thyself" is a direct, vital way of saying what Immanuel Kant said more formally in his statement of the Categorical Imperative: "So act as to treat humanity, whether in thine own person or in that of any other, always as an end and never as a mere means."

The liberal is one for whom this principle is basic. For him, all measures are to be tested by their bearing upon persons, for persons are of primary and essential value. The state exists for man, not man for the state. Property exists for man, not man for property. No man or group may rightly be the mere slave or chattel of another. The liberal is against all human exploitation and for the common welfare. He favors only such use of the power of the state as is necessary to afford the conditions for the free development and exercise of the powers of persons.

The liberal believes in education rather than in regimentation by propaganda or by mere conditioning. He seeks the settlement of issues by reason rather than by force or violence. He is open-minded to new truth and ready to learn from experience; but he is not credulous of new fashions and proposals just because they are new. He has faith that beneath all our greed and sin and madness mankind is sound at heart and fundamentally reasonable; and if he is a Christian liberal or a Jew who has not forsaken the ancient wisdom of his people, he has faith in the justice, love, and power of God.

Faith is the other great characteristic word of the New Testament. Like the word "love," it appears about two hundred and fifty times.

There is a famous definition of faith in the New Testament. The writer of the Epistle to the Hebrews gives it: "Faith is the substance of things hoped for, the evidence of things not seen." We are truer to the meaning of his Greek if we use active verbs in place of the copula "is." Faith gives substance to our hopes; it proves what we do not yet see. Faith is a principle of action. It faces toward the future. It helps create the good toward which we strive. Faith is that present quality of purpose, of courage, of persistence that is indispensable if we are ever to make great hopes come true. It inspires that loyalty which Josiah Royce described as "the willing and practical and thorough-going devotion of a person to a cause."

There is a common notion that faith is the antithesis of knowledge, that it is concerned with a different set of objects, and that a clear line can be drawn between the things that we can know and the things in which we can only have faith. These notions are mistaken. Faith is not a substitute for knowledge or a rival to knowledge. It is a way of using knowledge. It is based upon knowledge, and it directs and applies knowledge to the accomplishment of high purposes.

Faith goes beyond assured knowledge, of course. It is of the very essence of faith to have courage, to venture, and to dare. Faith demands no antecedent pledge of security, no guarantee of success. Faith inspires creative action that outruns certainty and that is often directed to ends that are too great to be achieved in anyone's lifetime.

Never more than today has mankind needed that steadfast, vital union of love and hope and faith that is the spirit of the liberal. And never before have men and women of this spirit faced so great an opportunity and responsibility for the creative deed that new conditions of world citizenship require. A new birth of freedom for all mankind is possible in our time.

It has been the fashion for men schooled in the realism of politics to ignore or even to sneer at moral factors as irrelevant to international relations. But the truth is that all lasting relations of mankind rest upon foundations of right and good, upon justice and mercy, upon love and faith. Society cannot be organized upon the shifting sands of vices.

That may be tried and may stand for a while–it has been tried in our own day–but in due time, the society that is founded upon wrong will fall.

A just and durable world peace cannot be made; it must grow. All that peace treaties and international organizations can do is to afford conditions favorable to its growth. Among the foremost of these conditions, needed everywhere, is faith–faith that is willing to venture beyond assured self-interest to responsible partnership for the good of all, faith that faces the facts and counts the cost but that will not give up its conviction that what ought to be can be; faith in the fundamental honesty and reasonableness of mankind; faith that cuts through differences of color, culture, and creed; faith in justice and goodwill; faith in the almighty power and the unconquerable love and the healing grace of God.

This college has been dedicated throughout its history to liberal education. We honor the faith of its founders, not by mere repetition of their ways, for we must live in our own time, but by new victories of their spirit. And education today and tomorrow, as yesterday, becomes fully liberal, emancipating, effective only as together with knowledge and intellectual competence it begets faith and hope and love.

8

GIVE US THIS DAY OUR DAILY BREAD

Matthew 6:11

It is sometimes said that this is a strange petition to stand right in the middle of the Lord's Prayer. Before it are three petitions that are concerned with God–with reverence for His name, the coming of His kingdom, and the doing of His will. After it are three that are concerned with our moral needs and duties–with forgiveness for sin and failure, strength to meet temptation, and deliverance from evil. Between these, it seems to stand alone, a frank natural request for food.

Many attempts have been made to interpret this petition in more spiritual terms. Origen, in the third century, declared that when we repeat it we pray for "the spiritual bread which nourishes our spiritual being." In an eleventh-century manuscript of the New Testament, Jesus is made to say, "Give us this day for bread the word of God from heaven." In the Douay Version of the New Testament, the petition reads: "Give us this day our supersubstantial bread."

We do not know exactly the meaning of the Greek adjective that is translated by the English word "daily." It appears only twice, in the Lord's Prayer as recorded by Matthew and again as recorded by Luke. It is an adjective that is derived either from the verb that means *to come* or from the noun that means *being* or *essence*.

From the beginning, Christian scholarship has favored the derivation from the verb *to come*. The bread for which we pray is our bread for the coming day, and in the old Latin translation of the Scripture, this was expressed by the Latin adjective that means "daily."

But St. Jerome, when revising this translation in the fourth century, did a strange thing. He changed the adjective in Matthew's account of

This sermon appeared in *Best Sermons*, edited by Paul Butler, 1947. It is used here by permission of Harper and Row, Publishers.

the Lord's Prayer to *supersubstantialem* but left the word for "daily" unchanged in Luke's account. There is no good excuse that can be given for that. His action only shows that even saints can make mistakes.

The great liturgies of the Roman Catholic Church have continued, all through the centuries, to use the phrase "daily bread" and have never adopted Jerome's innovation. There is general agreement among scholars, and in both Catholic and Protestant usage, that the petition refers to God's material provision for the on-going of human life.

There was an odd debate, however, in the 1870s, when the King James Version was being revised by Committees of British and American scholars. Because the phrase means literally "bread for the coming day," it was suggested that the petition ought to be translated "give us this day our bread for the morrow." This issue was thoroughly discussed, and in the end, the proposal was rejected. Against it stands the fact that the Greek language has a definite word for the morrow that is used in the Sermon on the Mount and undoubtedly would have been used here if that meaning had been intended. Perhaps the decisive factor in the debate was that some of the protagonists of the suggested change went too far by proposing the translation,"give us tomorrow's bread today." That sounded so impatient and grasping as to seem ridiculous.

In the meetings of the Committee for the Revised Standard Version, this issue was debated again, and the decision was to retain the phrase that has been used through the centuries–"daily bread." We felt that it would be a mistake to try to date that bread too precisely. After all, the point to the petition is not that we are trying to set the hour when bread shall be delivered or asking God to keep our pantries supplied a day ahead of actual need; our prayer is that the regular provision for our physical needs may be maintained and the material conditions of life be unfailing.

So understood, this petition surely is appropriate to the Lord's Prayer. And it stands properly where it does, at the point where we turn in thought from God's sovereignty to man's duty. If God's will is to be done on earth as it is in heaven, it must be done by people. And people must live, capable in body and mind, if they are to fulfill God's gracious purpose for them. The Christian faith is for this world as well as for heaven; it is concerned with people's bodies as well as with their souls.

When we pray for daily bread, it is not because we are uncertain of God's disposition or feel that it is necessary to beg Him for His gifts. The prayer is simple recognition of His Fatherhood and of our dependence upon Him. "Your Father knows what you need before you ask Him," said Jesus as he began to teach this prayer to His disciples. When we say,"Give us this day our daily bread," we declare our faith that life and its sustaining are God's gift, and we express our trust in His constancy and our gratitude for His love.

Yet God's gifts are not realized by the idle; they must be sought, cultivated, produced, and distributed by people. The development of the sciences and the arts, the practice of sound economics and effective politics, and the putting of these to the service of social justice and goodwill are essential to the fulfillment of this prayer.

We must never forget that the Lord's Prayer deals with more than our individual need. It is not "*My* Father. . . Give *me* this day *my* daily bread." It is "*Our* Father. . . Give *us* this day *our* daily bread." We can offer this prayer sincerely only as we identify ourselves with the needs of all mankind and are willing to labor as well as to pray that all may have their fair share of God's good gifts. And God's gifts provide for more than mere subsistence; they include all that is necessary for the development of individual persons in fulfillment of their birthright as children of God.

Shortly before his death, William Temple, Archbishop of Canterbury, formulated a brief statement of six objectives that Christians should set before themselves and labor to secure. I want to give you that statement. It sets forth what the prayer for daily bread includes, under the conditions of life today, in the thought of one of the greatest of the Christian ministers and statesmen of our time.

1. Every child should find itself a member of a family housed with decency and dignity, so that it may grow up as a member of a happy fellowship unspoiled by underfeeding or overcrowding or dirty and drab surroundings.
2. Every child should have the opportunity of an education so planned as to make possible the full development of his powers.
3. Every citizen should have an income that will enable him to maintain a home and bring up children in such conditions as these.
4. Every citizen should have a voice in the conduct of the business or industry which is carried on by means of his labor, and the satisfaction of knowing that his labor is directed to the well-being of the community.
5. Every citizen should have sufficient leisure and rest to enable him to enjoy a full personal life with such interests and activities as his tasks and talents may direct.
6. Every citizen should have assured liberty in the forms of freedom of worship, of speech, of assembly, and of association for special purposes.

Underlying this statement of six objectives, Archbishop Temple insisted upon the principle that "The resources of the earth should be used as God's gift to the whole human race, and used with due consideration for the needs of the present and future generations."

The Lord's Prayer is compact, but it means a great deal. And when we pray in these days for daily bread, we ought to mean no less than the full range of necessities for the life of free persons that Archbishop Temple has outlined. Our use of that prayer is not simply a petition; it is also a dedication of ourselves to live and labor for its fulfillment. We cannot use any part of the Lord's Prayer without praying that God's will may be done on earth as in heaven. And that prayer is a pledge that we will ourselves seek sincerely to do His will, that we will never be content simply to receive but will labor to produce and will give and share, and that all people may have their just portion of His good gifts.

9

AND PETER

Mark 16:7

My text is very short–just two words: "and Peter." They are part of Jesus' first message to His disciples after His resurrection as recorded in the gospel of Mark: "Go, tell his disciples and Peter that he is going before you to Galilee; there you will see him, as he told you."

These two words have dropped out of Matthew's record of the message. That is natural enough; they had no special meaning for him. But Mark's gospel is based upon the reminiscences of Peter; and to Peter, these words meant everything. They had brought to him the assurance of Jesus' forgiveness.

Peter was the boldest of the twelve men who were Jesus' close friends and chosen disciples. He was so bold as even to think that he could plan better than his Master. He was the first to declare: "You are the Christ, the Son of the living God." Then when Jesus began to tell of the path of suffering and death that lay before him, Peter rebuked Him: "God forbid, Lord! This shall never happen to you." And Jesus turned and spoke to him more sharply than he ever spoke to any other of His disciples: "Get behind me, Satan! You are a hindrance to me; for you are not on the side of God, but of men."

But Peter's boldness persisted. When Jesus said at their last supper that His disciples would fall away that night and be scattered, Peter answered, "Even though they all fall away, I will not." Jesus said, "This very night, before the cock crows twice, you will deny me three times." But Peter answered vehemently: "If I must die with you, I will not deny you." And they all said the same.

Peter took a sword with him, and in the garden of Gethsemane, he struck out with it in defense of his Master and desisted only at Jesus' command. When they led Jesus away, he was the only one of the

---

This text was originally delivered as an Easter sermon.

disciples who followed. He kept on, up the street, through the gateway, right into the courtyard of the high priest's house; and there he unobtrusively joined the group of guards and servants who sat about the fire. He would not forsake Jesus; he was still hoping that he could do something to aid his Master. Certainly, when the time came, he could make again the good confession: "He is the Christ, the Son of the living God."

But that was not to be. Years later, he would stand before councils and potentates and bear witness to his Lord, and finally he would nobly die a martyr's death. But this night he got no such opportunity. It was a servant maid and an idle bystander who questioned him. What right had they to strip him of his anonymity? What good would it do to tell them of his faith? So, like any good spy in the enemy's territory, he lied. Once, twice, he denied his identity. When pressed for the third time, he let out an oath and began to swear. "I do not know this man of whom you speak."

Then a cock crowed. Peter remembered what Jesus had said. And he went away and wept bitterly.

His grief may have been touched with chagrin. It is the little, unsuspected things that trip men. And Peter had been caught unawares. But I think his sorrow was too bitter for that. He wasted no thought upon the silly servant or the idle loafer who had been his undoing. He was aghast to realize that he had done just what he had so firmly declared that he would not do, just what Jesus had sorrowfully said that he would do. He had denied his Lord!

We do not know where Peter was or what he did for the next two days and nights. Judas hanged himself. Peter was of sterner stuff, but he was overcome by remorse and buried in despair. Then, early on the morning of the first day of the week, comes the word from the tomb: "He has risen, he is not here. . . . Go, tell his disciples and Peter. . . ."

"And Peter." Just two words, but what glorious words! They made all the difference that words can ever make. We can imagine that Peter could hardly believe them at first. "Did he really say that?" he may have questioned. "Are you sure that he mentioned me?" "Yes, Peter, we are sure." Then Peter must have wept again, but now his eyes are shining with tears of joy. No wonder that many years after when, an old man nearing the end of life, he dictates to Mark his memories of Jesus, Peter still cherishes these words that everyone else had forgotten.

We do not know how the resurrection of Jesus took place, and it is useless to speculate. We have not the data upon which to base an investigation by the methods of modern science.

But there is one thing of which we are sure, one fact that is incontrovertible and that was of basic significance for all subsequent human history. The sorrow of Jesus' disciples was changed by what they saw and heard into gladness and joy and bold, unshakable faith. The resurrection became the basis of their preaching; and the Christian church, with all of its distinctive beliefs and practices that are so different from those of either Judaism or paganism, is the lasting evidence of their belief in Jesus, not as a dead Master but as the living Lord.

The reason for their joy was not merely that a resurrection had taken place; they had believed, like others of the Jewish people, in the resurrection of the dead, and they had seen resurrections in the course of Jesus' ministry. It was not that Jesus was restored to them, for he did not return to the early companionship that they had been privileged to enjoy. It was not that he set up the Messianic kingdom for which they had hoped, for he did not do that.

Their joy was because they suddenly awakened to the meaning of it all. They saw in the resurrection of Jesus an act of God, declaring to be true all that Jesus had taught them. This was to them the breaking in of eternity, affording them a vision of the infinite dimension in which their lives were set and had meaning. It brought to them a new relation to God, a new way of conceiving life, and a new power to live in the spirit of Christ. It made possible to them the beginning here and now, in this present world, of the sort of life that belongs to eternity. In this sense, as the Second Letter to Timothy puts it, the risen Jesus brought life and immortality to light.

There are some very dreary religions in the world and some very dreary definitions of religion. The worst, perhaps, is that of Salomon Reinach, who defined religion as "a set of scruples impeding our faculties." No less dreary is Bertrand Russell's description of the free man's worship as unyielding despair, cherishing his ideals, for their little day, in the face of the tramping march of blind, omnipotent power. But Christianity is different from these. Christianity is a religion of joy, of hope and faith and trust in the love of God. "If God is for us," says Paul in that magnificent passage in the letter to the Romans, "who is against us?. . . . Who shall separate us from the love of Christ? Shall tribulation, or distress, or persecution, or famine, or nakedness, or peril, or sword?. . . No, in all these things we are more than conquerors through him who loved us. For I am sure that neither death, nor life, nor angels, nor principalities, nor things present, nor things to come, nor powers, nor height, nor depth, nor anything else in all creation, will be able to separate us from the love of God in Christ Jesus our Lord."

Religion is far more than a name for our devotion to ideals; it is faith in *God's* disposition toward them and toward us. The issue at stake, as Professor Montague of Columbia University once put it, is "whether the things we care for most are at the mercy of the things we care for least." And the Christian answer is that the things we care for most lie close to the heart of God and that God's love for all persons is like the love that was in Jesus Christ. "The Omnipotence behind the universe is our Father and our Friend."

This does not mean that God consults our whims and grants our wishes. It is silly to expect Him to surrender wisdom and abdicate justice in order to indulge our petty and crude desires. It is not the things that we want but what we *ought* to want that are His concern. There are some things fit to be eternal, and there are many that are not. All that we can reasonably expect of the will of God, which is the ordering frame of the universe, is that there be opportunity for the perpetuation and progressive realization of life's higher values.

And life's higher values cannot be perpetuated or realized apart from the existence of persons. There are no such things as values in the abstract. Goodness, truth, beauty, justice have no worth as mere concepts or ideas. It is only as they are made concrete in the life of persons that they have value.

A year or two before his death, Professor William James replied to a questionnaire that some student of the psychology of religion had sent him. In answer to the question "Do you believe in life after death?" he wrote: "I have always believed in it, but I have never counted much upon it, until recent years. I think the reason I am counting on it now is that I feel I am just getting fit to live."

The major premise of the Christian belief in immortality is what Christ has shown us of the character and disposition of God. Its minor premise is the worth of persons. Kant's basic principle of ethics is grounded in the purpose of God Himself: "So act as to treat humanity, whether in thine own person or in that of any other, in every case as an end, and never merely as a means."

Concerning the details of life after death, we know only what we can infer from these general premises of faith. But there is no need to know more. It is enough if we can say with Whittier:

To one fixed trust my spirit clings;
I know that God is good.

I know not what the future hath
Of marvel or surprise,
Assured above that life and death
His mercy underlies.

I know not when His islands lift
Their fronded palms in air;

I only know, I cannot drift
Beyond His love and care.

One inference concerning the conditions of eternal life we can affirm with a fair measure of certainty. Eternal life is the life of persons existing in social relation to one another and in common allegiance to God. It cannot be that persons are simply absorbed into the being of God, for that would mean loss of identity and value. It cannot be that they simply rest in contemplation or pleasurable satisfaction, for that would mean that their continued existence would be without moral value. "The nearest thing to Heaven that we can attain on earth," says Canon Streeter, "is in the experience of love and fellowship, of the complete harmony of mind with mind and heart with heart, between those who feel themselves to be lifted out of and above themselves, not only by the depth of their personal affection but by their passionate devotion to some common interest or ideal." If that be true, as I am sure it is, we may best think of Heaven as the full realization of such fellowship in the presence of God, without the hampering of evil, and with endless possibilities of good.

The best treatment of this subject that I know is in the chapter on "The Goal of the Moral Life" in Professor A.E. Taylor's *The Faith of a Moralist*. Let me quote from it a sentence or two in which he discusses the question of whether or not the absence of evil means that there is nothing left to do. "The moral life would not disappear even from a world in which there were no wrongs left to be righted. Even a society in which no member had anything more to correct in himself, and where 'Thou shalt love thy neighbour as thyself' were the universally accepted rule of social duty, would still have something to do; it would have the whole work of embodying the love of each for all in the detail of life. . . . There is no reason why the disappearance of wrong. . . should put an end to adventure and novelty. . . . There would be no more progress *towards* goodness of environment or character, but there might be abundant progress *in* good, onward movement in the manifestation of the principle of the good life in even more varied and richer forms."

It is this vista of the infinite dimension of the good life that began to open before the disciples on Easter day. They now knew that what they had seen in the face of Jesus Christ was the light of the knowledge of the glory of God. They found themselves standing, not at the end of a happy episode, but at the beginning of eternal life.

To one of the disciples the Easter message brought all this, and more. It brought also a personal message of forgiveness. "Tell his disciples and Peter." Surely there is significance for us all in the fact that the risen Lord did not forget Peter and that He not only remembered but cared to send to Peter this word. It is evidence of the love that will not let us go.

Death is never the last word. Neither are sin and failure the last words. There is always the chance to go on, to begin again, to forget what lies behind, and to press forward to what lies ahead. Easter stands not only for the historical fact that issued in the founding of the Christian church and not only for the faith in eternal life that undergirded and strengthened it but also for a personal, individual message of forgiving and redeeming love.

10

INTRODUCTION TO HORACE BUSHNELL'S CHRISTIAN NURTURE

Horace Bushnell's *Christian Nurture* is as significant today as when it was published one hundred years ago. Modern psychology and sociology have confirmed its insights, and the best of modern education is in its spirit. It is, moreover, still interesting and easy to read.

With the possible exception of some of Jonathan Edwards' writings, no American book can with better right be deemed a religious and educational classic. *Christian Nurture* sharply challenged the extreme individualism, the reliance upon emotional revivals, and the arbitrary supernaturalism that had characterized the thought and practice of most of the American churches from the middle of the eighteenth century. But its message is positive and constructive rather then merely critical, and much of that message is timelessly true.

Bushnell was no local figure merely. He lived in New England, but his influence reached far beyond the New England theology that he inherited, criticized, and transformed. Men who knew and cared little about it eagerly read him. And whether they differed or agreed with what they read, they acknowledged the fresh, creative quality of his mind. He was one of those forward-looking souls to whom it is given to help make the world different, to move it appreciably away from what has been toward what may and ought to be.

Like other men of action and of creative mold, Bushnell was accused of overhaste. It was once said of him that he wrote and published first, then read up on the subject afterward. Of this book, at least, that is not true. A lifetime of experience and study went into the writing and rewriting of *Christian Nurture*. As a young pastor and a

This is the introduction written by Luther Weigle as editor of the centenary edition of Horace Bushnell's *Christian Nurture*, published by the Yale University Press in 1947.

father, he began early in his ministry to face the problem with which it deals. In 1838, he published an essay on "Spiritual Economy of Revivals of Religion," and six years later another entitled "Growth, not Conquest, the True Method of Christian Progress." He was invited, in 1846, to discuss the subject before the ministerial association of which he was a member. The two "Discourses on Christian Nurture" that he delivered in response to this invitation were published by the Massachusetts Sabbath School Society, but the publication was suspended and the book withdrawn from sale a few months later because of the opposition it aroused. He then republished the "Discourses" in1847, together with a spirited "Argument" in their defense, the two earlier essays, and two sermons upon related themes. Finally, in 1861, he wrote the book upon the subject that remains a classic in its field.

When Bushnell began his ministry, the prevalent theology in many of the New England churches was, in temper and spirit, a heritage from the Great Awakening of 1740-42, under the powerful preaching of Jonathan Edwards. Doctrines akin to those of Edwards had crystallized into an orthodoxy, and the corresponding practices had become established as the custom of the churches through successive waves of emotional religious revival. The arbitrariness of God's sovereignty was stressed. Overemphasis was laid upon the dogmas of original sin and total depravity. Man's inability was his most discussed attribute; and it was held that even the prayers of unconverted folk render them odious in the sight of God, for these are manifestations of their self-love. One's only hope lies in a conversion and self-surrender so complete as to involve a willingness to be damned for the glory of God. Yet no one can make this surrender of his own will or can by any striving experience conversion. It is the gift of God to those to whom he pleases to grant it; it is entirely the work of the Holy Spirit. There are no "means of grace," strictly speaking, for no human action or desire can make a soul one whit more sure of ultimate possession of the regenerating grace of God. These old New Englanders took in sober earnest the text that likens the Spirit to the wind–"thou canst not tell whence it cometh and whither it goeth." There was nothing for them to do except to realize their lost condition and to hope that God might choose, in His own good time, to grant them His converting grace. This grace manifested itself usually in seasons of revival; yet even revival meetings could not be planned for and "put on." They might be desired and prayed for, but their coming depended wholly upon the will of God.

There was no hesitation about applying these principles to children. They, too, were held to be lost in sin, depraved by nature, and in need of a wholly new heart. They were children of wrath until the Holy Spririt should transmute them into children of God. It mattered nothing what their parentage or what the quality of the home in which they were brought up. All alike, whether the children of Christian parents or of open sinners, were considered to be partakers of the common heritage of guilt and alien to the kingdom of God, until such time as He should grant them a new birth. Older folk can do nothing for them, then, save to seek to deepen in them a sense of their need and to pray on their behalf for the gift of conversion.

Here, then, was a practical issue facing the young minister. What attitude shall he take toward the children? Debating this in his own mind year after year, in the light of his experiences as a pastor and as a father, he began to distrust revivals, in spite of the measure of value in them that he did not deny, and more and more to trust the influences of family life in a Christian home. He could not believe that emotional excitement is necessary to conversion or that it is a test of religious character, and he could not believe that the influences of family life make no difference within the child or in the sight of God. He came finally to feel that the current theory and practice were fundamentally wrong and untrue to the laws of nature and to the purposes of God.

In opposition to the current theory and practice, Bushnell formulated what he held to be the true idea or principle of the Christian education of the young, "that the child is to grow up a Christian, and never know himself as being otherwise. . . . In other words," he went on to explain, "the aim, effort and expectation should be, not, as is commonly assumed, that the child is to grow up in sin, to be converted after he comes to a mature age; but that he is to open on the world as one that is spiritually renewed, not remembering the time when he went through a technical experience, but seeming rather to have loved what is good from his earliest years."

He defended this thesis with a wealth of argument that rests ultimately upon two propositions: that the nature of the family as a social group is such that the spirit and character of the parents inevitably influence the life and character of the children and that the life of the family may thus be a means of grace in that it affords an instrument that God may use for the fulfillment of His promises and constitutes a natural channel for the power of the Holy Spirit.

The first of these propositions is psychological. The essential truth of Bushnell's position on this point, which he terms "the organic unity of the family," is abundantly confirmed by modern psychological and sociological investigations of group behavior; of child development; and of the factors contributing to nervous disorganization, mental disease, and moral delinquency.

The second of Bushnell's propositions is theological. It asserts a relation between the natural and the supernatural to the study of which he devoted a whole volume before he wrote the final edition of this book. That his position is better and truer theology than the arbitrary supernaturalism that it displaced is generally agreed. The laws of nature are not recalcitrant. They belong to God, not to evil.

In all this, Bushnell remained on distinctly evangelical ground. He had no quarrel with the idea that human nature has been corrupted by sin. He agreed that man is of his own strength unable to realize the possibilities of good that lie before him by the grace of God, and he believed that man's supreme need is for the converting, regenerating power of the Spirit of God. But he held that the current views put undue and unreal limitations upon the work of the Divine Spirit. God's hand is not so shortened that He cannot save except at revival meetings; His Spirit is not bound so that He cannot use the natural laws and forces that He has ordained. Rather we should expect to find in these natural laws and forces the accustomed instruments of God's working upon the lives of men; they constitute the wonted channels for the empowering grace of the Holy Spirit.

The final rewriting of the book, published in 1861, added a second part, which is devoted to practical counsels concerning the training of children in the Christian family. To come down to details is always perilous, but Bushnell did it successfully. This section of the book reflects the experience of a father as well as the convictions of a Christian minister. It is as concrete as the better books of today on child-training, and it has more body and substance than many of them because its counsels are underlaid by a consistent philosophy of life and of religion, instead of being a mere collection of devices that have chanced to work.

It is remarkable how the shrewd insight and wholesome common sense of this man, joined to his Christian devotion, anticipated much that more scientific methods of observation have now established with respect to the up-bringing of children. Physical nurture, he held, may be a means of grace; one cannot be a Christian in his mind and not be a Christian in his body. He asserted the unity of the psychophysical organism and propounded a Christian doctrine of eugenics long before these terms came into use. He stressed the importance of the early years of childhood in a way that is quite in line with what we are learning about the preschool child. He believed that more, as a general fact, is done, or lost by neglect of doing, with respect to the character of the child in the first three years of life than in all the years of discipline afterward. He pointed out the implications of the habits of eating, exercise, and dress into which children are permitted to fall, and found in such matters as the regularity with which a baby is fed, simplicity of diet and of dress, and good manners and wholesome conversation at the table important factors in the development of moral and religious character.

There are strong chapters dealing with problems of family discipline, family worship, and the Christian teaching of children in the home. In all, the principle followed is the same. It is the Christian life of the parents, their good sense, and the completeness of their own devotion to the will of God as shown him in Christ that matter most. Parental government is genuine, and parental authority real, to just the extent that the parents themselves are governed by God, take His purposes for their own, and seek to make their home a dwelling place of His Spirit. Family prayer is natural if it brings to conscious expression the aims of the family's everyday living; it is artificial, forced, and ineffective if "it stands alone in the house, and has nothing put in agreement with it." It is easy to teach children the principles of Christian truth, provided this teaching is but an explanation to them of the motives that actually determine the behavior that they see and the conditions of life that they share. "You teach Christ not by words only, but by so living as to make your own life the interpreter of his."

Bushnell opposed what was called "indoctrination," which consisted chiefly in the memorization of dogmatic catechisms, and favored a larger emphasis upon the understanding of Scripture; he advocated the grading of methods and materials of instruction in Christian truth; he recommended greater freedom in conversation with respect to the objects of religious belief and more sincerity in answering children's questions and in dealing with adolescent doubts; he believed that the play of children, instead of being a symptom of original sin, is a "divine appointment" of educative value; he conceived the goal of education in terms of what he called the "emancipation of the child."

All this is modern. No part of Bushnell's work is more generally accepted today, no body of his ideas is more alive and functioning than the principles enunciated in his successive articles and books upon the subject of Christian nurture. The chief criticism now raised is that he expects too much of parents, who, in these days at least, have not the intellectual competence nor the religious devotion nor the available time to carry out the program he proposed.

Here, for example, is a complaint concerning the impracticability of such parental nurture under the stress of modern life. The writer pictures the tired businessman coming home to meet a wife worn out with social and domestic duties. "The weary comes home to the weary —the careworn meets the careworn. The pressure upon a multitude of business and professional men is really frightful; combined with the necessity of going long distances to their places of duty, it produces little short of an absolute separation from their families. There are fathers in our community who are almost strangers to their own children—who do not know one-half as much about them as their schoolteachers. The appropriate work and play and worship of the home cannot be so much as begun in many dwellings, and anything is caught at which promises to relieve parents from work which they can find no time to do."

The date of that complaint is 1860! It was published the year Bushnell wrote the final draft of *Christian Nurture*. The frightful pressure it describes was in the good old hectic days of the horse and buggy. There always have been indolent, incompetent, and spiritually inert parents. There were such in Bushnell's time, and there are such now. But in no time is it impossible for parents to afford their children the wise and loving nurture that this book describes.

The first two chapters of this book are the original "Discourses," which Bushnell left unchanged because, he said, "under the fortune which befell them, they had become a little historical." The fourth chapter was added when the "Argument" was published in 1847; and the other thirteen chapters were written for the final publication in 1861. The fourth, fifth, and sixth chapters were written from the standpoint of the churches that practice infant baptism; but the central principles of Christian nurture are valid also for churches that dissent from this practice and admit to baptism only those mature enough to profess their own faith.

In 1916, in connection with the establishment at the Yale University Divinity School of the Horace Bushnell Professorship of Christian Nurture, a new edition was published. At the request of Mrs. Dotha Bushnell Hillyer, who endowed this chair in memory of her father, the text was revised by the excision of a few brief passages of a controversial sort. Their omission in no way affects the argument. They were stricken out because lines of division are no longer drawn as they once were nor do those who might dissent from Bushnell's argument bear the same party names. At the same time, the analytical table of contents was added.

The present centenary edition of *Christian Nurture* is published in celebration of the one-hundredth anniversary of the original publication and in response to the demand that a book so important should not go out-of-print. A brief biographical sketch prepared by Williston Walker for the 1916 edition is retained.

The preparation of a bibliography of Bushnell and of the growing body of literature concerning him is a major task that will in due time be undertaken. Meanwhile, the reader is referred to *The Life and Letters of Horace Bushnell*, by Mary Bushnell Cheney, New York, 1880, second edition, 1903; *Horace Bushnell, Preacher and Theologian*, by Theodore T. Munger, Boston, 1899; *Minutes of the General Association of Connecticut–Bushnell Centenary*, Hartford, 1902; and the excellent article on Bushnell by Charles A. Dinsmore in *The Dictionary of American Biography*. The best study of the setting of Bushnell's doctrine of Christian nurture in the Calvinistic heritage is by Lewis B. Schenck, *The Presbyterian Doctrine of Children in The Covenant*, New Haven, 1940.

appendix

I should like to append to this volume of memorabilia two pieces of a personal nature.

The first is a sketch of my mother, Clara Boxrud Weigle, written in 1965 as a birthday gift for my father the year after her death. Her influence upon his life and career is incalculable.

The second is a letter written to my father for Valentine's Day, 1975, preserving family tales and traditions for his children and grandchildren.

It is my hope that the general reader too may gain here a more intimate understanding of this remarkable man—his genuine goodness, his intellectual power, his generous ways, his abounding vitality, his zest for life, and his enduring faith.

Ruth Weigle Guyton

"OVER THE RIVER AND THROUGH THE WOOD TO GRANDMOTHER'S HOUSE WE GO!"

Another July, another journey—from Hanging Moss Creek, heavy with silt and Mississippi midsummer heat, up fifteen hundred miles of highway to the hills of New Hampshire, where the streams rush sparkling over the tumbled rocks. Sunapee! "First to see the lake!" all the children shout as we round the curve by the Granliden, and the dear, familiar first glimpse of the lake erases the aches and weariness of three days' waiting. Turn deep into the woods, pungent with the scent of balsam and of pine. Follow the winding road, dappled with late afternoon sunlight sifting through the birches. "There's the sign!" "Here's Grandpa's road!" and suddenly, we have arrived at journey's end.

Here is the cottage, brown-stained shingles with green-painted trim, still snug through forty winters' weight of snow, still welcoming through forty summers the children home, and now their children. The pink spirea stand, graceful sentinels at either side of Grandma's flower garden; the window boxes are brave with bright geraniums, pink begonia, white impatiens, and trailing blue lobelia. The door swings wide, and here is Grandpa, meeting us with arms outstretched. And here is Johnny, safely arrived ahead of us, from science camp in West Virginia. Why are we waiting now at the threshold; what is the strange reluctance holding us back? Till Tom, at three, the last and littlest of all the grandchildren, voices the question trembling unspoken on all our lips, "Where's Grandma?"

In the kitchen she must be, still baking for our coming–with deft, sure hand sprinkling sugar and cinnamon and melted butter on the plump dough; poking raisins in some, leaving some plain; rolling, pinching together, and slicing off the luscious chunks to fill the brown-sugar-and-butter lined pans. Is she sliding golden-brown loaves out of the oven, filling the whole house with the blissful smell of new bread baking? Or can she be holding a blueberry pie high on the fingertips of her left hand, while the quick knife in her right slashes off the overlapping crust the "leftover dough" to make a little brown-sugar pie for the youngest? Could she be fitting the last batch of oatmeal cookies, still warm, into the round red tin?

Perhaps she has carried the vegetables down to the little dock, to shuck the corn or slice the beans for supper while she dangles her feet like a girl in the cool water. Or could she still be there by the bank, in her old blue bathing suit, forgetting how late it grows as she bends to the endless task of picking up the sharp stones and sticks the winter's waves uncovered, determined to wrest a little sandy beach from an unwilling shore? Can it be warm enough that she might venture out to swim, breasting the waves with stately strokes, coronet of braids held high above the water like a crown?

No, it must be she has washed that wealth of dark brown hair, now frosted white at the temples. Is she sitting by the garden, combing and brushing the long strands for the breeze and the last late sun to dry?

This is her favorite spot, by the curving flower bed, an unexpected splash of color in the clearing, contained between the granite rocks she placed here, bordered with her prized maidenhair fern, the earth carried in, bit by bit, from the woods' rich decay, the flowers new planted each June–watered, weeded, fed and dusted, coaxed and tended into bloom.

Butterflies and hummingbirds will gather here from all the country round.

This kinship with the earth and all good growing things–is it the bequest of her Norwegian mother and father and their forbears in that stern, beautiful land not unlike this very New England? Surely from them she learned the thrift that saves the coffee grounds for mulch each morning to sprinkle about the yard in faithful ceremony; that buries the eggshells, the melon rinds, the pea pods with the wood stove ashes to nourish the sparse soil of the hillside vegetable patch. Adamant optimist, she will not give up, though never yet has a tomato ripened before first frost, nor have all the rolls of chicken wire fencing ever foiled the depredations of the woodland creatures–woodchuck, porcupine, and rabbit. Indeed, one huge and hoary rabbit has become the family pet with years of early-morning nibbling. "Bunny-Bun" the children and Grandma call him, watching with equal delight for his dignified return each summer. Who could begrudge a tender meal to such a stouthearted fellow, grave survivor of how many New Hampshire winters?

Can you hear her swift light step about the house, hurrying with the last preparations for our coming? "Clara is so quick," her mother used to say, half-proud, half-rueful. Perhaps she is laying the clean, sweet-smelling towels on the bathroom racks, marking each rack with its user's name. Maybe she is smoothing the last spread, bringing extra quilts and blankets from the zinc-lined windowseats to cocoon these Mississippi children against the chill night air. Could she be uncovering the toys in the big attic–the bottletop collection, the designs of colored beads, the blocks and pegs, the miniature cars–all the treasures of two young generations, and more, for there is no object more beloved than the ancient croquinole board, Great-Grandfather and Great-Grandmother Weigle's birthday gift to little Luther Allan, September 11, 1885.

Perhaps she is setting the table for thirteen with the yellow pottery plates and the amber glasses. Who else but Grandma can stretch house and heart to welcome so many with such joyous ease! David, Robert, and Johnny share the cardtable with her. Grandpa presides at one end of the waxed birch table; I minister to Tom in the high chair and keep order at the other; Jeannie, Doug, and Jim sit in a row on the cushioned window seat side, while Cathy, Steve, and Arthur pull in their chairs opposite.

It may be she is lighting a fire in the huge stone fireplace to cheer us at the supper table. The big boys' job will be to keep the logs piled ready in the giant splint woodbasket she discovered upcountry in Vermont and contrived miraculously to carry home in the car. The little ones will gather sticks and twigs in the woods for Grandma's kindling box. First Sunapee waking sound for forty years has been the iron stove lids rattling while Grandma lights the kitchen fire; then, if the morning's cold, the crackle and spit from the living room hearth, where Grandma will have a fine blaze going by getting-up time for all the sleepy shiverers to huddle by and dress before.

But is it evening news time? Then we shall find her by the radio in her room, hand on the dial, as she listens to the late reports, her mobile features reflecting her keen concern. Call her old-fashioned, if you will. Use outmoded words like "rectitude" and "virtue," "character" and "integrity"—she weighs the world in exacting scales, but remember, each judgment will be tempered with love. If the news is over, she will be reading in the living room while she waits, creaking the rocker softly as she turns the pages. When we surprise her, she'll pull off the dark-rimmed reading glasses, and we will be dazzled by the radiance in those great blue eyes.

"But where *is* Grandma?" the little voice grows more insistent. "Hush, Tom, she isn't here. Grandma is dead," Cathy ventures to explain.

It was just here, by the back door, where we left her that early August morning. She had been put to bed the week before—it was her heart that could not keep the pace her vivid spirit set. This morning she disobeyed her orders and came out to see us off; a slight, indomitable figure in her white, crinkled nylon dress, waving good-by until we rounded the hilltop out of sight. Both of us knew it was the last time—we'd known all summer without acknowledging it, even to ourselves. "I don't care what it costs," she laughed when we demurred the price of summer theater tickets she insisted we accept. "I made up my mind before you ever came, we'd just enjoy this visit and not think of what it costs!" There was another leavetaking, in the hospital three weeks later, when I returned alone, but this was the real good-by, here at the threshold where we stand now.

"But who will keep care of us?" the uncertain small voice quavers. Looking down, I see the troubled brown eyes cloud, and I can hesitate no longer.

"Why, Tom, I will. That's what a mother's for. Here, take my hand. We've supper to fix, beds to make, the fire to light. Tomorrow we'll get down the toys. Come on, Sugarfoot! Let's go inside."

Epilogue

High on a New Hampshire hilltop, in the shelter of a giant pine, all that was mortal of Clara Boxrud Weigle was laid to gentle rest September 8, 1964. Her shining spirit is in God's keeping. The simple stone in the North Newport cemetery reads:

Luther Allan Weigle
1880-19
Dean of the Yale University Divinity School
Clara Boxrud Weigle
1885-1964
Gracious Friend. Beloved Wife. Devoted Mother
Love Never Ends 1 Cor 13.8

LOVE LETTER

Dear Daddy, February 10, 1975

Here it is, nearly Valentine's Day. Tom's English teacher is requiring him to memorize Elizabeth Barrett Browning's "How do I love thee? Let me count the ways." As I hear him recite, I am remembering Richard's words to Luther, Margaret, and me at Sunapee the night after Mother's death. You had "turned in"–to bed, if not to sleep, carrying with you a weight of private grief your children could not share. "Someday," Richard vowed, "someday, I'm going to find the words to tell that man just how much he means to me." Whether he has ever found those words, I do not know. I do know that every day his goodness and his faithfulness speak volumes. But what of me, your youngest? Can I find words to speak, while you are here to listen? How do I love you? Can I count the ways?

I love you for all you have achieved in ninety-five magnificent years as scholar, educator, author, administrator, churchman of the world.

I've heard your sermons many times, in many places, from Yale's majestic Battell Chapel to the backwoods New Hampshire church, where two home-grown geraniums in shiny tin cans adorned the altar, and your presence permitted the young student pastor and his bride a week-end honeymoon. I've been in your congregation on shipboard, crossing the Pacific. I've marched in cap and gown to hear you preach my Wellesley Baccalaureate. Each time I've felt like shouting, "Listen! That's my Father!"

I remember my wild dash across New York City from Kennedy Airport to the Interchurch Center on Riverside Drive, barely in time to surprise you as you started down the aisle for the service in your honor. Midwinter morning fog had delayed my flight from Mississippi. To convince the taxi driver of the necessity for all possible speed, I had tried to explain your role in the production of the Revised Standard Version. Awed but game, he careened around corners, gasping, "You mean he wrote all them books of the Bible!" An untutored tribute, as genuine as the eloquent words of the Archbishop of Hartford, conferring upon you the Knighthood of Saint Gregory by order of Pope Paul VI, in recognition of your contribution toward Christian unity in Biblical scholarship: "Surely it is no exaggeration and it is meant as no conventional compliment to say that Dr. Weigle has been a chosen instrument of the Lord for the historic task of bringing separated brothers together in the reading of the Word of God."

Accolades have accompanied your public career from the very first. Browsing through the Carleton College *Algol* for 1913, I discovered: "Among all the Carleton faculty there is none more universally admired and better liked than Dean Luther A. Weigle. As professor of philosophy, every member of his class is certain there can be none better. His magnetic personality and unusual gifts of concreteness make it easy for him to transform the obscure arguments of a Kant or Hegel into something intelligible. His philosophy is no mere matter of mental gymnastics but rather a living principle. . . .His popularity with the students, his wonderful executive ability and infinite capacity for work have served him in good stead as dean of the college. . . .Everyone who knows him is his friend."

Occasionally, your exuberance outran your dignity. Remember "The Faculty Meet" in that same yearbook?

> Place–Gridley Hall, 3rd Parlor
> Time–Monday evening, 7:25
> Enter–The Faculty, en masse
> Professor Weigle–"Hel-lo
> Miss Evans (Dean of Women and Social Arbiter)–"H'm–Good Evening, Dr. Weigle!"
> Dr. Weigle–"Oh! Good Evening."

No wonder the caption under that handsome picture of you in the

Prince Albert coat reads, "For Heaven's sake, I'll have to put the lid on my slang!"

Thirty-six years later, one of those Carleton students, Robert L. Calhoun, brilliant Yale Divinity professor of philosophy, recalled those early Minnesota days, "Looking back now, I am tempted to say that the same qualities so familiar to the Divinity School and to thousands of its constituents and friends, were already visible to any shrewd observer: the same amazing capacity for work, the same inclusive friendliness and good humor, the same easy competence in administration and in all sorts of human relations, and the same zest for the whole diverse enterprise of education. . . .Dean Weigle's perceptiveness, patience, fairness and resourcefulness in the conduct of the common business of the school I have not found equaled in any other moderator I have known."

Another of the stars on your Divinity faculty was that colorful Methodist preacher and wit, professor of homiletics, Halford E. Luccock. His tribute at your retirement is typically unique:

"You put your money on my coming to Yale when it was a frightful risk–in racing language, a 1 to 100 shot! I have always been a risk, but I would have completely fallen down and rolled over on the track if it had not been for your constant encouragement and backing. That is for the record for St. Peter at the pearly gates, and I will tell him all about it.

"More than that, has been the continuous pleasure of working with you, the sheer fun of it. For with the work and responsibilities and often anxieties you have had–a load of them that would have flattened out three other men, you always came up with a good humor that, to me, has been one of the wonders of the world. As was said of Job, 'Your words have kept men on their feet'–this man, particularly.

"You will remember my telling you this morning of my seeing the Twenty Mule Team and its driver as a youngster in St. Louis. You have had a twenty-man team to urge forward. I do not mean that the faculty have been mules. But it has called for skillful driving, just the same. You have kept the team in the traces and working together for a long pull. And the record of your achievement has been unparalleled in America. That is one of my understatements, no fooling.

"Thank you for living."

On your ninetieth birthday, you were still being thanked.

The President, Fellows and Faculty of Yale University

extend their affectionate greetings to
the Reverend Luther Allan Weigle

on the occasion of his Ninetieth birthday. The University community remembers his service with deep appreciation and his scholarly eminence with pride. Dean of the Divinity School for over two decades and Sterling Professor of Religious Education until his retirement in 1949, he has filled the intervening years with preparation of the new Revised Standard Version of the Bible, a distinguished combination of modern scholarship and literary sensitivity.

Reuben A. Holden
Secretary

When you reached ninety-five, President Brewster himself wrote: "Your perdurability is exceeded only by the quality of your service to this University and the affection in which you are held in this community."

Such is the public Luther Weigle; there is another, private Luther Weigle whom I love for all you are to your family. If Mother was the heart of the family, you are its head. Together, you made "home" the richest word in the English language to your children. Looking back I realize it was your love for each other, freely and confidently expressed, which gave us this happy security.

I never tired of hearing how you and Mother met and courted. You were a young professor at Carleton. It was registration day in September 1906. Clara Rosetta Boxrud had spent her junior year at Wellesley, but, fortunately for the course of these events, Wellesley would not accept all of her high school credits, insisting upon an additional year to complete college requirements. Being an independent young woman, Mother simply returned to Carleton, to graduate with her class of 1907. There she was, with those sky-blue eyes, asking whether she might take your course in Christian Ethics. "I wanted to tell her she could take anything she liked with me," you'd always say with a grin.

Because it was not deemed proper for a faculty member to single out one of his students, you waited until the year was nearly over before you asked her to accompany you to a literary society dinner. She accepted, but, oh disaster, in clumsy eagerness you let her slip off the boardwalk into the mud, bedraggling the new gown and feather boa! Still, you were a persistent chap. Things must have gone better, for at a graduation picnic, someone snapped a picture of you and Clara, sitting back to back.

That was the summer you spent in Europe, traveling with your father and thinking about Clara for two long months, without hearing from her. In Rome, you bought her a pearl necklace. Upon returning, you went to the little Minnesota town where she was teaching school and surprised her with the pearls. "Oh, Luther," she exclaimed, flushing with excitement, "they are so beautiful! How can I ever thank you?

I'm just going to give you a great big–a great big–handshake!" You didn't get that kiss until you'd proposed and been accepted.

Then Clara's mother tried to make her change her mind. Clara was the first of the four daughters to want to marry. To Jennie Boxrud, Clara was too young; she hadn't known you long enough; better reconsider. But you knew it was time to be masterful. All Clara's qualms were tenderly but firmly overruled. A promise was a promise, you told her, and that was that. She finished her year of teaching, spent one year at home acquiring all the housewifely arts, and on June 15, 1909, she became your wife.

Together you shared fifty-five years of a happiness only a few experience. She died in 1964; yet the house is still alive with her presence. On every side, you are surrounded with evidence of the perfection of her ways–her taste and foresight, her care for your comfort, and her love. Many times you've told me, "I thank God every night for Clara, for the blessing she has been to me, through the years–and still is!"

Mealtimes were good family times. Always you pronounced the familiar blessing: "Our Heavenly Father, we thank Thee for this food. Bless it to the strengthening of our bodies and us to thy loving service. Help us in all things to do Thy will. In Jesus' name. Amen." One particularly busy day, you came home for lunch, hard-pressed between engagements. The telephone calls at your office had been unusually harassing. Just as we were seated, the telephone rang again, for you. You went to answer, telling us to go ahead. When you returned, we bowed our heads and folded our hands for the delayed blessing. Into the expectant hush came, strong and clear, "Mr. Weigle speaking." We weren't really surprised; we'd always known you had a direct line with the Almighty!

What talk and laughter we shared! Remember the Pennsylvania Dutch stories? Because you had grown up in that part of the country, you came by the dialect as naturally as breathing. We'd beg to hear about the noodle factory, how one day a stranger stepped from the train at the station. Looking about inquiringly, he took a few hesitant steps, first in one direction, then in the other. Finally, he ventured to approach one of the local inhabitants lounging idly on the corner. "Beg pardon, sir," he asked, "could you direct me to the spaghetti factory?" "Spaghetti factory?"puzzled the native. "I didn't know ve had a spaghetti factory." The stranger thanked him and started down the street to seek information elsewhere. The native turned to a friend who walked up and said, "Dot man vanted de spaghetti factory. I didn't know ve had a spaghetti factory." "Maybe he means de noodle factory," suggested the friend. "Dot's right," agreed the native and ran down the street after the stranger. "Hey, mister! Hey, mister! Vas dot de noodle factory you vanted?" "Yes, that's right, the noodle factory," the stranger replied expectantly. "Vell," said the native, "I don't know vere dot is neider!"

You'd reach your peak performance as the train conductor on the Reading Line who was breaking in a new man to the job. It was the new chap's first day, and he was understandably nervous. "Don't vorry," the conductor reassured him. "Chust listen to me, young fellow, and call out vot I do de same sing." The train departed; the first station approached; the conductor opened the door at one end of the car and called, "Besslehem, Besslehem next stop. All out here for Besslehem. Change cars for Souss Besslehem, Bass, and Nazzarass!" The new man opened his door with a flourish, drew a deep breath, and bellowed out at his end of the car, "Same sing at zis end; same sing at zis end!"

Always the meal concluded with your hearty thanks to your wife, the cook. No man was ever more appreciative, nor had better cause to be. As Roland Bainton has well said, your Clara was a "culinary artist." Every now and then, when supper was over, you'd propose to all assembled, "Let's go to the movies!" Off we'd rush, leaving the dishes in the sink, to make the seven o'clock show at the Pequot Theater. We never checked to see what the film might be. In those days, it wasn't necessary. Pot luck was part of the fun.

Sundays we'd line up, six strong, in a front pew at the Church of the Redeemer. Mother's sweet soprano mingled with your fine bass, singing "Holy, Holy, Holy, Lord God Almighty," "Ancient of Days, Who Sittest Throned in Glory," "The Church's One Foundation," and all the rest. One particular hymn, "O God, Our Help in Ages Past," I shall associate always with Yale commencements. As dean, you received choice tickets for the ceremonies. Year after year, it was thrilling to see the famous candidates for honorary degrees and listen to Billy Phelps's eloquent citations. I remember his capsule description of Walt Disney, "the man who labored like a mountain and brought forth a mouse." Each commencement I'd beam with pride when you stepped forward to declare, "Mr. President, I have the honor to present to you the candidates for the degree of Bachelor of Divinity."

New Haven meant Yale, and school; Sunapee meant summer, and freedom—and the best family time of all. What a journey it was, back and forth—at least a five-hour trip in the big open Studebaker touring car, with the luggage strapped on the running boards, along with a crate or two of chickens, according to Mother's fancy. The little folding seats were the choice positions. Dick would play the harmonica, while the rest of us would sing. To revive us, Mother would dole out squares from a Baker's German sweet chocolate bar. Occasionally, for a treat, we might lunch at Wiggin's Tavern in Northhampton; more often it would be a picnic in the Yale forest, with Mother filling every spare container with the clear, cold spring water. There were favorite filling stations, favorite vegetable stands, and always the debate over the best route–Brattleboro or Keene. The family would go up in June, as soon as school was out, though you'd be commuting back and forth weekends until midsummer, when you could come to stay till Labor Day. The horn would honk at the top of the hill to announce your arrival Friday nights. Up we'd rush to help lug down the sacks of vegetables, the stack of books and magazines and mail. By the next morning, you'd be wielding the axe again or plying the two-handled saw with one of the boys, cleaning up your woods and stocking the woodshed. Margaret and I never relished the invitation you'd issue on these occasions, "Girls, come be beef!" This meant, of course, to steady the log with our weight while you sawed–not the most flattering proposition. But whatever the work, it was the stuff dreams are made of, and there at Sunapee, the family made a dream come true.

If Sunapee was the family's special place, Christmas was the family's special season. It would all begin on Christmas Eve. Once the evening meal was over and the dishes were done, we'd gather by the fire to hear you read *The Suitable Child,*[1] *Home for Christmas,*[2] or "The Man Who Missed Christmas."[3] These were our favorites, and before you finished, each of us would have wiped away a surreptitious tear or two. Then came the ritual of laying our packages for each other under the tree, each one pretending he couldn't see the others. Next morning we assembled in the upstairs hall, to descend together, littlest to biggest, in that rank. Stockings first, before breakfast. The packages under the tree were not to be opened until the morning tasks were done. Then one of the family served as Santa Claus, handing round the gifts, one by one, each member of the family sharing the surprise and pleasure of the others. My Christmas gift to you was invariably the same–a small pocket diary and engagement calendar. Each year you contrived to exhibit complete astonishment and satisfaction in the gift. Christmas dinner always included foreign students from the Divinity School who had nowhere to go for the holidays. We children used to grumble some between ourselves at these intrusions, then suffered pangs of shame to see the gratitude and joy of the invited guests. In just such ways you stretched the world for us.

Most of all, you opened the world to us in books. We grew up in a paradise of books. You'd start us out with *'Fraid Cat,*[4] *English Fairy Tales,*[5] *The Pig Brother,*[6] *Ameliaranne and the Green Umbrella,*[7] and *Stories to Tell the Littlest Ones.*[8] For years, I never bothered with a public library. Everything I could read or need was on the shelves at home. From you, I learned to value words, written and spoken. From you, I acquired the habit of looking things up. How many times I'd see you stop whatever you were doing or saying to check the *Britannica, Who's Who,* or *Webster's Unabridged*! Although I never shared your crossword puzzle passion, I did catch another one of your addictions–your predilection for a good detective story. Between us, we must have read all of J.S. Fletcher, Agatha Christie, Manning Coles, Josephine Tey, and Andrew Garve.

Public figure, family man, whatever the role, you've played the part with zest and high good humor. I love you for what Hal Luccock called "the sheer fun of it." With that irrepressible twinkle, you declare, "I always said I'd never be the sort of old man who complained the world was going to the dogs–but then, I never really thought it would!" Back in your Carleton days, the students named you "Leather-lunged Luther." You appointed yourself unofficial, volunteer cheerleader, adapting Yale cheers to Carleton athletic events, till every student knew Boola-boola, and the entire college could sing "March, march on down the field, fighting for Carleton!" You played the banjo; you sang bass in the Glee Club; you joined the tennis team, coached the debaters, emceed the banquets, conducted vespers, inspired, admonished, and astonished the undergraduates. The story goes that you were intercepted once on campus by a brash young student with a far-fetched request. Your response became a Carleton classic, "Young man, your request is so absurd that I am going to grant it as a reward for your nerve."

Another choice student story dates from the Divinity School of the '30s when it was against the rules for students to keep food or cook in their rooms. Two roommates were tidying up after a forbidden breakfast. One opened the window and shook out the tablecloth. The other remonstrated with him, warning, "You'd better not do that. The dean is likely to see you." "If he does," his friend retorted indignantly, "I'll tell him those crumbs are for the birds, not for an old buzzard." As if to punctuate the reply, there was a knock on the door. The culprit opened it to find you standing there. He seemed quite nonplussed as you extended an invitation to both students to have Christmas dinner at our home. Some years later, the whole story came out, for the joke was too good to keep. No one got more amusement out of the entire proceeding than you did.

The tale I love the most comes from the 1928 International Missionary Council in Jerusalem. This was one of the great meetings of Christendom. Out of this meeting ultimately evolved the World Council of Churches. Delegates were attending from all over the world. The agenda was to be handled by means of preliminary papers, distributed for study to all delegates prior to the conference. You and Dr. J. H. Oldham had written the paper on Religious Education, a pamphlet of about eighty pages.

John R. Mott was presiding. When this paper came up for consideration, an English delegate rose to protest. The paper was too long, too complicated, too confused; it used words that were too big; it was unintelligible; he had read it three times on the way to the meeting and still could not make head or tail of it. He urged that this paper on Religious Education be scrapped and another be written, a simple paper of about twenty pages, using simple words, for this was a simple subject.

There you sat, appalled, praying for grace not to make a fool of yourself, when suddenly a champion arose, and there was no need for you to say anything at all. Up stood a huge black delegate in a long black frock coat, Professor Dickinson Don Tengo Jabavu, of Fort Hare College, South Africa. "Mr. Chairman," he declared, "I cannot hear language like this without making a protest. I have read this article and I understand every word of it. What's more, there are one hundred and fifty black teachers just like me in my district and they've read every word of it. In fact, they've prepared a written study of this article as their contribution to this meeting. Mr. Chairman, I hope you don't prepare a simpler article on this subject. But if you do, send it to England. Don't send it to Africa. We don't need it." Down he sat, to thunderous applause.

Those were the glory days. Now life has narrowed to the limits of an upstairs room, but thousands the world over hold you in their hearts and lift you in their prayers. How do I love you? Who could count the ways? I love you for the courage with which you face the diminution of your powers. I love you for the twinkle with which you still greet adversity. I love you for the steadfastness with which you stay the course. I love you for the confidence with which you know the end is only a beginning.

---

[1]Norman Duncan, Fleming H. Revell Co., 1909.

[2]Lloyd C. Douglas.

[3]The Christmas Heretic and Other Stories, J. Edgar Park, Pilgrim Press, 1926.

[4]L. J. Bridgman, Philadephia, George W. Jacobs & Co. Publishers, 1913.

[5]Joseph Jacobs, N.Y. and London, G.P. Putnam's Sons, The Knickerbocker Press, 3rd ed rev., 1889.

[6]Laura E. Richards, Boston, Little Brown & Company, 1919.

[7]Constance Heward, Philadelphia, George W. Jacobs & Co., Publishers, 1920.

[8]Sara Cone Bryant, Houghton Mifflin Co., 1916.

LUTHER ALLAN WEIGLE

bibliography

(in order of appearance)

I. Books

The Pupil and the Teacher. Philadelphia, Pa.: The United Lutheran Publication House, 1911 (London: Hodder & Stoughton; New York: Doran; Boston: Pilgrim Press, 1911), pp. 217.

New edition, copyrighted 1929, with revised questions for discussion and new bibliographies at the end of each chapter. This remained in print until 1942.

Abridgements of Part I, *The Pupil*, and Part II, *The Teacher*, for use in teacher-training classes, were published in separate paperback volumes, from 1916 on, by the United Lutheran Publication House, the Pilgrim Press, and other denominational publishing houses in the United States and Canada.

Translations of *The Pupil and the Teacher* into Chinese, Japanese, Portuguese, and Spanish were published and used in churches and missions in lands where these languages were vernacular. An example of these translations is *Curso preparatorio para los maestros, traducido al Espanol por Domingo B. Castillo*, published in Nashville, Tenn., E.U.A. by *Casa Editorial de la Iglesia Metodista Episcopal del Sur, Lamar y Barton, Agentes, 1924.* In this volume Part I, *El Discipulo*, and Part II, *El Maestro* are translations of *The Pupil and the Teacher.*

Another example is *El Discipulo: Un estudio de la psicologia de la ninez y la juventud. Texto aprobado por el Comite Central de Education Religiosa para el Curso Normal Oficial. Santiago De Chile Imprenta Universitaria*, 1927.

Editor: *Christian Nurture*, by Horace Bushnell. Revised edition with an analytical table of contents and a biographical sketch by Williston Walker. New York: Charles Scribner's Sons, 1916, pp. xxx + 351.

Training the Devotional Life (with Henry Hallam Tweedy). New York: Doran, Boston: Pilgrim Press, 1919, pp. 96.

Talks to Sunday School Teachers. New York: Doran, 1920, pp. 188.
This volume contains articles published monthly, from January 1918 to December 1919, syndicated in *Pilgrim* magazine. This volume was translated into Portuguese for the use of Baptist churches and missions in Brazil. It was published as *Palestras com os Professores da Escola Dominical*, by *Casa Publicadora Baptista,* Rio de Janeiro, 1930.

The Training of Children in the Christian Family. Boston, Chicago: The Pilgrim Press, 1922, pp. 224.

American Idealism. New Haven: Yale University Press, 1928, pp. 356. (The Pageant of America, Vol. X.)

We Are Able. New York and London: Harper & Brothers, 1937, pp. 98.

Jesus and the Educational Method. New York, Cincinnati: The Abingdon Press, 1939, pp. 128. (The James Sprunt lectures at Union Theological Seminary in Virginia, 1938.)

Editor: *Christian Nurture*, by Horace Bushnell. Centenary edition, with an introduction by Luther A. Weigle. New Haven: Yale University Press, 1947, pp. xi + 351.

The English New Testament from Tyndale to the Revised Standard Version. New York: Abingdon-Cokesbury Press, 1949, pp. 158. Edinburgh: Thomas Nelson & Sons, pp. viii + 150. 1950. (Based on a series of Cole lectures at Vanderbilt University.)

The Living Word: Some Bible Words Explained. New York: Thomas Nelson & Sons, 1956, pp. 72.

Bible Words in Living Language. Edinburgh: Thomas Nelson & Sons, pp. x + 100, 1957. (British edition of *The Living Word*.)

The Bible Word Book, Concerning Obsolete or Archaic Words in the King James Version of the Bible, by Ronald Bridges and Luther A. Weigle. New York: Thomas Nelson & Sons, 1960, pp. x + 422.

The New Testament Octapla: Eight English Versions of the New Testament in the Tyndale-King James Tradition. With eight plates of title-pages. Edited, with introduction, by Luther A. Weigle. New York: Thomas Nelson & Sons, 1962, pp. xvi + 1489.

The Genesis Octapla: Eight English Versions of the Book of Genesis in the Tyndale-King James Tradition. With eight plates of title-pages. Edited, with introduction, by Luther A. Weigle. London, New York: Thomas Nelson & Sons, 1965, pp. xiv + 301.

II. Brochures

Luther and the Protestant Reformation. A quadricentenary program for Reformation Sunday. Boston, Pilgrim Press, 1917.

Home Training and the Problem of Authority. Nashville: General Sunday School Board of the Methodist Episcopal Church, South. Bears the imprint also of the educational boards of ten other denominations, 1923, pp. 8.

The Church and Christian Education. American Section. Report of Commission Five to the Universal Christian Conference on Life and Work, held in Stockholm, Sweden, August 19-30, 1925. New York, Universal Christian Conference on Life and Work, 1925, pp. 40.

Religious and Secular Education. New York: American Tract Society, 1927.

The Spiritual Training of Children. Program Outlines and Suggestions for State and Local Chairmen of Committees. Washington, D.C.: The National Congress of Parents and Teachers, 1928, pp. 16.

The Teacher of Religion and the Problem of Authority. Convocation Address, Boston University, School of Religious Education and Social Service, January 30, 1930. Boston, pp. 15.

The New Paganism and the Coming Revival. Richmond, Va., Executive Committee of Religious Education and Publication (Southern Presbyterian Church), 1931. Also published in *Yale Divinity News,* 27, no. I: 1-2, November 1930; *Yale Alumni Weekly*, 40: 201-202, November 7, 1930; Federal Council Bulletin, 14: 6-8, April 1931.

Public Education and Religion: An Address Delivered at the 1940 annual meetings of the International Council of Religious Education before the Joint Conference of the Professional Advisory Sections on Wednesday, February 7, 1940, at the Stevens Hotel, Chicago, Illinois. Chicago, Ill.: International Council of Religious Education, 1940, pp. 18.

Christian Education Today. Report of the Committee on Basic Philosophy and Policies, edited by Luther A. Weigle, chairman. The International Council of Religious Education. Chicago, 1940, pp. 40.

America's Heritage of Faith. Commencement Address at Carleton College, June 4, 1945. Published by Carleton College, 1945, pp. 12.

An Introduction to the Revised Standard Version of the New Testa-

ment, by members of the Revision Committee. Luther A. Weigle, chairman. New York: Thomas Nelson & Sons, 1946, pp. 72.

An Introduction to the Revised Standard Version of the Old Testament, by members of the Revision Committee. New York: Thomas Nelson & Sons, 1952, pp. 92.

Bible Words that Have Changed in Meaning. New York: Thomas Nelson & Sons, 1955, pp. 36.

Church and State in America. Social Action, published by the Council for Social Action of the Congregational Christian Churches, Vol. XIII, No. 9, November 15, 1947. pp. 5-14.

III. Articles in Books

"Supplementary Report of the Commission on Religious and Moral Education," in The National Council of the Congregational Churches of the United States, sixteenth regular meeting, New Haven, Conn., October 20-27, 1915. Boston, 1915, pp. 412-436.

The Encyclopaedia of Sunday Schools and Religious Education. Three volumes. New York: Thomas Nelson & Sons, 1915.
"Attention, How to Secure and Hold," Vol. I, pp. 61-65.
"Creeds, Place of, in Religious Education," Vol. I, pp. 315-318.
"Culture Epoch Theory," Vol. I, pp. 322-323.
"Examinations," Vol. I, pp. 392-393.
"Habit," Vol. II, pp. 504-505.
"Interest and Education," Vol. II, pp. 556-561.
"Lesson Previews," Vol. II, pp. 628-629.
"Recapitulation Theory," Vol. III, pp. 862-864.
"Review and How to Conduct It," Vol. III, p. 921.

"The Effect of the War upon Religious Education," in *Religion and the War*, by members of the faculty of the School of Religion. Yale University, ed. by E. Hershey Sneath. New Haven: Yale University Press, 1918, pp. 105-121.

"Report of the Commission on Moral and Religious Education," Minutes of the National Council of Congregational Churches of the U.S., Grand Rapids, 1919, pp. 246-254. Also published in the *Church School*, December 1919.

"The Educational Service of the Christian Churches in the Twentieth Century," in *Education for Christian Service*, by members of the faculty of the Divinity School of Yale University; a volume in commemoration of its one hundredth anniversary. New Haven: Yale University Press, 1922.

"Departments of Religious Education in Theological Seminaries," in *Organized Sunday School Work in North America, 1918-1922.* Chicago, International Council of Religious Education, 1922, pp. 427-432.

"The Teaching Work of the Church." The Committee on the War and the Religious Outlook (appointed by the Federal Council of the Churches of Christ in America). New York: Association Press, 1923. Chapters 1 and 2 were drafted by Luther A. Weigle.

"Conferences Conducted by the Joint Advisory Committee on Materials and Methods for Religious Education on the Foreign Field," in *The Sunday School and the Healing of the Nations: The Official Book of the World's Ninth Sunday School Convention*, held in Glasgow, Scotland, June 18-26, 1924. New York: World's Sunday School Association,'1924, pp. 126-130.

"The Place of Religious Education in Church Programs," in Proceedings of the Council of Cities of the Methodist Episcopal Church, 7th annual meeting. Philadelphia, 1924, pp. 90-99.

"Recent Experiences in Lesson Course Making in North America," in Proceedings of the Council of Cities of the Methodist Episcopal Church, 7th Annual Meeting, 1924, pp. 278-287.

"The Church and Education," in *Christianity and Social Adventuring*, ed. by Jerome Davis. New York: Century Co., 1927, pp. 257-273.

"Contribution of Religion to Education." Chap. V in *Parents and Teachers: A Survey of Organized Cooperation of Home, School, and Community*, prepared under the auspices of the National Congress of Parents and Teachers and ed. by Martha S. Mason, Boston, New York (etc.), Ginn & Co., 1928, pp. 90-110.

"Beginning at Jerusalem," in *Thy Kingdom Come,* the official book of the World's Tenth Sunday School Convention, held in Los Angeles, Calif., July 11-18, 1928. ed. by John T. Faris, New York, World's Sunday School Association, 1928, pp. 335-340.

"Religious Education" (with J. H. Oldham). Chap. I in *The Jerusalem Meeting of the International Missionary Council,* March 24-April 8, 1928, Vol. II: *Religious Education,* pp. 1-89. New York, London, International Missionary Council, 1928. Also sole author of Chap. VII in the same volume: *Christian Religious Education,* pp. 171-180.

"What is a Christian College?," in *Addresses Delivered on the Occasion of the Inauguration of Edmund Davison Soper as the Seventh*

President of Ohio Wesleyan University, Thursday and Friday, February 14-15, 1929, Delaware, Ohio, Ohio Wesleyan University, 1929. pp. 3-16.

"School and Curriculum: the United States: Religion," in *Encyclopaedia Brittanica*, Fourteenth Edition, Vol. 20, pp. 92-92. New York: Encyclopaedia Brittanica, Inc., 1929. London, Encyclopaedia Brittanica Co., Ltd.

Dean Weigle's address (at the one hundred and twenty-fifth anniversary celebration of Monson Academy). In Monson Academy, Monson, Mass., 1804-1929. One hundred and twenty-fifth anniversary, June 8, 1929, pp. 5-14. Monson, Mass. Board of Trustees, 1929.

"What Makes Religious Education Christian?" pp. 118-121. "Taking Time for Christian Education," pp. 234-236. "Go. . .teach: Report of the Quadrennial Convention of the International Council of Religious Education," Toronto, Canada, 1930. Chicago: International Council of Religious Education, 1930.

"Objectives of a Christian College," in *The Inauguration of Clarence Moore Dannelly as President of Kentucky Wesleyan College*, pp. 5-17. Winchester, Kentucky Wesleyan Press, 1930.

"The Need of Commitment to a Living Lord," in *Finding the Will and Power of the Living God,* Report of the Annual Spiritual Emphasis Conference held at Lake Mohonk Mountain House, Mohonk Lake, N.Y., October 15-16, 1932, under the auspices of the Commission on Message and Purpose of the National Council of the Young Men's Christian Associations of the U.S.A. New York: Association Press, 1932, pp. 22-27. Message and Purpose Paper, No. 7.

"The Religious Education of a Protestant," in *Contemporary American Theology: Theological Autobiographies,* ed. by Vergilius Ferm, New York: Round Table Press, Inc., 1932-33, Vol. 2, pp. 309-340.

"The Purpose and Plan of the Convention," in *The Living Christ in the World Fellowship of Religious Education.* The official record of the World Sunday School Convention held in Rio de Janeiro, July 25-31, 1932. St. Louis: Published for the World Sunday School Association by the Bethany Press, 1933, pp. 49-53.

"The Purpose of Missions," Chap. VIII in *The Christian Message for the World Today.* New York: Round Table Press, 1934, pp. 166-181.

Education for Service in the Christian Church in China, ed. by Chester S. Miao. Shanghai and New York: 1935. Report of a survey and conference, of which Dean Weigle wrote Chaps. I, II, and IV-VI, pp. 99-105, 110-135. Published in New York by Board of Founders, Nanking Theological Seminary.

"Religious Education and School Administration," in *Educational Progress and School Administration,* ed. by Clyde Milton Hill. New Haven: Yale University Press, 1936, pp. 329-344.

"Christ the Hope of the World," in *Christ the Hope of the World: The Twelfth World's Sunday School Convention,* Oslo, Norway, July 1936, pp. 200-208.

"Christ and the Bible in Education." in *Christ and the Bible.* A series of six addresses delivered at the 1937 Northfield General Conference as a feature of the D. L. Moody Centenary Celebration; with an introduction by Dr. John McDowell, chairman of the D. L. Moody Centenary Executive Committee. East Northfield, Mass.; The Northfield Schools, 1937.

"Theological Education," in *Interpretative Statistical Survey of the World Mission of the Christian Church,* summary and detailed statistics of churches and missionary societies, interpretative articles, and indices, ed. by Joseph I. Parker. New York, London: International Missionary Council, 1938, pp. 250-252.

Articles on "Sunday Schools" in the successive annual volumes of Brittanica Book of the Year, 1938-1946. New York: Encyclopaedia Brittanica.

"Today's Message," March 19 and December 1, in *The Spiritual Diary; A Day-by-Day Inspirational Guide.* New York: Jordan House, 1940.

"Christian Education and World Evangelization," in *Christian Education and World Evangelization: Official Report of the International Congress of Christian Education,* Mexico, D.F., Mexico. New York: World's Sunday School Association, 1941, pp. 12-17.

"The Religious Background of Democracy," in *Science, Philosophy, and Religion: Second Symposium.* New York, 1942, pp. 540-548.

"Christian Motivation Supplies an Essential Prerequisite to Effective Action," Chap. IV in *A Righteous Faith for a Just and Durable Peace,* published by the Commission to Study the Bases of a Just and Durable Peace, John Foster Dulles, chairman. New York: Federal Council of Churches, 1942. pp. 104 (Chap. IV, pp. 27-31).

Articles on "Church Membership," successive annual volumes of Brittanica Book of the Year, 1942-1946. New York: Encyclopaedia Brittanica.

Biographical articles concerning Francis Edward Clark, Benjamin Fay Mills, Dwight Lyman Moody, Henry Clay Trumbull, and Milton

Valentine, in the appropriate volumes of the *Dictionary of American Biography.* New York: Charles Scribner's Sons, 1943.

"A Personal Confession of Faith," in *The Quest for God through Faith.* A book of credos on the vital experiences and significant values of life, for use in worship services and discussion groups especially for young people in churches, church schools, young people's meetings, summer camps and institutes, Y.M.C.A. and Y.W.C.A., and for leaders and counselors of young people. Wyoming, Ill.: Press of the Post-Herald, 1944, pp. 75-77.

"Religious Liberty in the Postwar World," in *Religion and the World Order: A Series of Addresses and Discussions,* ed. by F. Ernest Johnson. New York: Institute for Religious Studies; distributed by Harper, 1944, pp. 29-37.

"The American Tradition and the Relation between Religion and Education," in *Religion and Public Education: Proceedings of a Conference,* Washington, D.C.: American Council on Education, 1945, pp. 26-34 (American Council on Education. Studies, Ser. 1, Reports of Committees and Conferences, No. 22, Vol. IX, February 1945).

"The Courage to Be Liberal," in *Education and the Faith of America: Address Given During the Centennial Celebration of the Packer Collegiate Institute.* Brooklyn, N.Y., 1945.

"The Revision of the English Bible," in *Biblical Scholarship and Religious Education: A Symposium.* Mendota, Ill; 1946, pp. 67-70. (from *Religious Education*, XLI).

"The Challenge of the Future: An Outside View," in *Methodism,* ed. by William Ketcham Anderson. Cincinnati: Methodist Publishing House, 1947, pp. 291-299.

"Give Us This Day Our Daily Bread," in *Best Sermons,* ed. by Paul Butler. New York and London: Harper & Brothers, 1947, pp. 250-255

"The Aim and Scope of Religious Education," in *Orientation in Religious Education,* ed. by Philip Henry Lotz. New York: Abingdon-Cokesbury Press, 1950, pp. 87-98.

"Thirty-five Years of Co-operation in Theological Education," in *To Do and to Teach: Essays in Honor of Charles Lynn Pyatt.* Lexington: The College of the Bible, 1953, pp. 65-73.

Articles on "The Revised Standard Version of the Bible," in the successive annual volumes of Yearbook of American Churches, 1953-

1965, ed. by Benson Y. Landis. New York: National Council of the Churches of Christ in the U.S.A.

"English Versions since 1611," in *The Cambridge History of the Bible: the West from the Reformation to the Present Day*, ed. by Stanley Lawrence Greenslade. Cambridge, Eng.: University Press, 1963, pp. 361-382.

"The Standard Bible Committee," in *Translating and Understanding the Old Testament*, edited by Harry Thomas Frank and William L. Reed, a collection of essays by Old Testament scholars dedicated to Herbert Gordon May on the occasion of his retirement from Oberlin College. Nashville, Tenn.: Abingdon Press, 1970, pp. 29-41.

IV. Introductions, Forewords and Prefaces

Introduction to *Project Lessons on the Gospel of Mark*, by Nellie Content Kimberly Wadhams. New York, London; Century Co., 1925.

Introduction to *A Curriculum of Worship for the Junior Church School, First Year*, by Edna M. Crandall. New York: Century Co., 1925, pp. xiv + 364. Professor Weigle wrote further introductions to Vol. II, 1926, pp. xvi + 364 and Vol. III, 1927, pp. xviii + 364.

Introduction to *The Crisis in American Lutheran Theology: A Study of the Issue between American Lutheranism and Old Lutheranism*, by Vergilius Ferm. New York: Century Co., 1927.

Introduction to *The Kingdom of Love*, by Blanche Carrier. Garden City: Doubleday, Doran & Co., 1928.

Introduction to *Making the Bible Desired*, by Dorothy Dickinson Barbour. Garden City: Doubleday, Doran & Co., 1928.

Introduction to *Bible Stories Told Again*, by Howard R. Gold. New York, Chicago: Fleming H. Revell Company, 1929.

Introduction to *What Is Lutheranism? A Symposium in Interpretation*, ed. by Vergilius Ferm. New York: Macmillan, 1930.

Introduction to *Objectives in Religious Education*, by Paul H. Vieth, New York and London: Harper & Brothers, 1930.

Introduction to *Karl Barth and Christian Unity: The Influence of the Barthian Movement upon the Churches of the World*, by Professor Adolf Keller, translated in collaboration with Professor Werner Petersmann, by Rev. Manfred Mamody, and revised by Dr. A.J. Macdonald. New York: Macmillan, 1933.

Introduction to *Education for Life with God*, by Wilfred Evans Powell. New York: Abingdon Press, 1934.

Preface to *The Pilgrim Hymnal*, Boston and Chicago: The Pilgrim Press, 1935. Preface signed: Luther A. Weigle, chairman, Publication Committee.

Introduction to *God in Our Public Schools*, by W.S. Fleming. Pittsburgh, Pa.: The National Reform Association, 1942.

Introduction to *Crusade for Education: The Development of Educational Ideals in the Church of the United Brethren in Christ*, by Edwin H. Sponseller. Frederick, Md.: E.H. Sponseller, 1950.

Foreword in *A Picture-History of the Bible and Christianity in 1000 Pictures, with Inspiring Stories of all the World's Great Religions.* Los Angeles: 1952.

Introduction to *Our Public Schools–Christian or Secular*, by Renwick Harper Martin, D.D. Pittsburgh: The National Reform Association. 1952.

Introduction to *Alexander Campbell and His New Version*, by Cecil K. Thomas. St. Louis: The Bethany Press, 1958.

Introduction to *Reading the Bible Aloud*, by J. Edward Lantz. New York: Macmillan, 1959.

Introduction to *Prayers for Girls*, by Elizabeth Robinson Scovil. Camden, N.J.: Thomas Nelson & Sons, rev. ed., 1966.

Introduction to *Prayers for Boys*, by Herbert C. Alleman. Camden, N.J.: Thomas Nelson & Sons, rev. ed., 1966.

V. Articles in Periodicals

"Special and Conditioned Students in Colleges in the North Central Territory," paper read before the North Central Association of Colleges and Secondary Schools, Chicago, April 1914. Proc. 19th Annual meeting, pp. 79-87.

"The Psychological Basis of Worship," paper read before the Religious Education Association in New Haven, March 1914. *Religious Education*, IX, 419-424, October 1914.

"The Church Committee on Religious Education," *Augsburg S.S. Teacher*, XLII, 81-82, February 1916.

"Worship in the Sunday School," *Augsburg S.S. Teacher*, XLII, 147-148, 208-209, March and April, 1916.

"Bad Results of Inattention: How to Develop the Habit of Attention, *Christian Educator*, I, 151, 171-172; May and June, 1917.

"Our Religious Education in War-time, " *Pilgrim Magazine*, II, 339-341; *Pilgrim Elementary Teacher*, II, 305-307, June 1918.

"The Home Education of Children in Prayer," *Lutheran Church Work and Observer*, April 24, 1919.

"The Christian Family," *Church School*, November 1919

"The Modern Home and Its Perplexities," *Church School*. December 1919.

"The Home Atmosphere," *Church School*, January 1920.

"Building Strong Bodies," *Church School*, February 1920.

"Forming Right Habits," *Church School*, March 1920.

"The Child at Play," *Church School*, April 1920.

"The Child at Work," *Church School*, May 1920.

"The Child at Study," *Church School*, June 1920.

"Developing a Taste for Good Reading," *Church School*, 22-25, 45, July 1920.

"The Child and His Friends," *Church School*, 22-26, August 1920.

"Doing for Others," *Church School*, 17-20, September 1920.

"Training the Devotional Life," *Church School*, 22-26, October 1920.

"The Child and the Church," *Church School*, 24-26, 46-47, November 1920.

"Training Children for Christ," *Westminster Teacher*, May 1920.

"Repentance." Holman Lecture for 1921 on the Augsburg Confession. *Lutheran Quarterly*, LI, 247-283, July 1921.

"What Constitutes Research in Religious Education?" *Religious Education*, XVI, 347-349, December 1921.

"Progress in Lesson Making," *Church School*, III, 444-448, July 1922.

"The Biblical Argument for Graded Lessons," *Church School*, IV, 52-54, November 1922.

"What Makes Education Religious?" *Religious Education*, XVIII, 90-92, April 1923.

"The Christian Ideal of Family Life as expounded in Horace Bushnell's

Christian Nurture." *Religious Education*, XIX, 47-57, February 1924.

"The Elimination of Religion from Public Education," *Christian Work*, CXVII, 254-255, 258, September 6, 1924.

"The Christian Education of American Children," *Union Seminary Review*, XXXVI, 215-241, April 1925.

"The Present Status of the Work of the International Lesson Committee," *Religious Education*, XX, 225-233, June 1925.

"Jesus Christ, Educator," *International Journal of Religious Education*, I, 9-10, September 1925.

"Religion and the Public School," *Federal Council Bulletin*, IX, 19-20, 30, January 1926.

"The Secularization of Public Education," *Religious Education*, XXI, 90-95, February 1926.

"What Is Religious Education," *International Journal of Religious Education*, II, 24-25, June 1926.

"A Survey of Contemporary Theological Education," *Bulletin*, 5th biennial meeting of the Conference of Theological Seminaries and Colleges in the United States and Canada, V, 11-18, September 1926.

"Greetings from Yale University," *The Lutheran Quarterly*, LVI, 513-525, October 1926.

"The Place of Religion in the Education of Children," *International Journal of Religious Education*, p. 14, October 1926.

"Why the Principle of Public Responsibility for Education Has Prevailed in the United States," *Religious Education*, XXII, 319-332, April, 1927.

"The Task Ahead, As I See It," *Religious Education*, XXII, 456-457, May 1927.

"Religion and the Public School," *Federal Council Bulletin*, X, 17-18, June 1927.

"What the Church Is Doing for Character Education, and What It Is Not Doing," *Religious Education*, XXII, 574-579, June 1927.

"The Public Schools and Religion: Facing the Menacing Results of Ignoring Religion in American Education," *Christian Advocate*, CII, 680-682, June 2, 1927. Reprinted in *Western Christian Advocate*, XCIII, 520-522, June 2, 1927; and in *Pacific Christian Advocate*, LXXII, 8-10, June 2, 1927.

"Educating Children in the Use of Money," *International Journal of Religious Education*, IV, 10-11, October 1927.

"Religious Education at the Jerusalem Conference," *International Journal of Religious Education*, IV, 16-17, 46, June 1928.

"Prayer as Fellowship: A Sermon Preached in Battell Chapel, Yale University, " *Congregationalist*, CXIII: 490-492, October 18, 1928.

"The Relation of Church and State in Elementary Education," *International Journal of Religious Education*, V, no. 2, 12-14, November 1928.

"What Is It to Be a Christian?" *Yale Divinity News*, XXV, no. 1, 1-2, November 1928.

"Religious and Secular Education," *Religion, The Dynamic of Education*, a symposium on religious education, ed. by Walter M. Howlett, pp. 9-25. New York and London, Harper & Brothers, 1929.

"Heritage and Responsibility," *Congregationalist*, CXIV, 405, 420, 421, March 28, 1929.

"Beginning at Jerusalem," *Workers' Council*, VI, no. 4, 2-3, April 1929.

"The Need for Trained Leaders," *Westminster Leader for the Church School*, II, no. 7, 10-11, April 1929.

"Where Is Authority?" *Yale Divinity News*, XXVI, no. 1, 1-2, November 1929.

"Some Characteristics of Jesus as a Teacher," *Record of Christian Work*, XLVIII, 736-740, December 1929.

"The Pope's Encyclical on Education: II–A Protestant Comment." *Current History*, XXXI, 1089-1090, March 1930.

"The Jonah Motive in Modern Life," *Congregationalist*, CXV, 645-646, May 15, 1930.

"Jesus as a Teacher," *Epworth Herald*, XLII, 235, 252, March 14, 1931.

"The Educational Standards of Theological Seminaries," Presidential Address, *Bulletin of the Seventh Annual Meeting of the Conference of Theological Seminaries and Colleges in the United States and Canada*, VII, 54-67, April 1931.

"The Child in the Midst," *The Lutheran*, XIV, no. 9, 3, November 26, 1931.

"Can Protestantism Endure?" *Federal Council Bulletin*, XIV, no. 9, 7-9, November 1931. Also printed in *Yale Divinity News*, XXVIII, no. 2, 1-2, January 1932, and in *The Christian, Kansas City*, VIII, 182-

184, January 30, 1932.

"Report of the Commission on the Message of the Conference," The fourth conference of the Christian Unity League, *The Christian Union Quarterly*, XXI, 235-237, January 1932.

"Who and What Determine the Educational Policies of the Theological Schools," Proceedings, 15th annual meeting American Council on Education, May 6-7, 1932, *Educational Record*, XIII, 201-211, July 1932.

"Address at the Dedication of the Sterling Divinity Quadrangle," *Yale Divinity News*, XXIX, 3-4, November 1932, and *Yale Alumni Weekly*, XLII, 54-56, September 30, 1932.

"Diplomacy of Retaliation Endangers Civilization," *Christian Evangelist*, LXIX, 1603, December 15, 1932.

"Resources of Men and Training," *Religion in the Preparatory Schools*, the proceedings of the National Conference of Preparatory School Masters, held at Atlantic City, N.J., October 7-9, 1932, ed. by B. Edwards and H.B. Ingalls, pp. 58-60. (Young Men's Christian Associations.) National Council of Student Christian Associations. Publication no. 1. New York, National Council of Student Christian Associations, 1933.

"The Coming Idealist," *Christian Evangelist*, LXX, 723-724, 738, June 8, 1933.

"The Laymen's Inquiry and Religious Education," *International Journal of Religious Education*, IX, 15, 24, June 1933.

"Training Leaders in China," *World Call*, 22-23, July 1936

"The International Sunday School Lesson System," *Union Seminary Re-View*, 180-189, April 1936.

"Contemporary Agnosticism," *Yale Divinity News*, XXXV, no. 1, 1-3, November 1938.

"Robert Seneca Smith," *Yale Divinity News*, XXXV, no. 2, 1, February 1939.

"The Duty of the Churches in the Present Crisis," *Yale Divinity News*, XXXVI, no. 1, 1-3, November 1939.

"A Review of *The Complete Bible: An American Translation*," *Christendom*, January 1940.

"New Books in American Church History," *Yale Divinity News*, XXXVI, no. 3, 3-5, April 1940.

"When Is Education Religious?" *Adult Student*, September 1940. Nashville, General Board of Christian Education, Methodist Episcopal Church, South.

"Democracy, Education, and Faith," *Yale Divinity News*, XXXVII, no. 1, 1-3, November 1940.

"Democracy, Education and Faith in God," *The Princeton Seminary Bulletin*, XXXV, no. 1, 7-14, August 1941.

"Charles Allen Dinsmore," *Yale Divinity News*, XXXVIII, no. 1, 1, November 1941.

"The Religious Foundations of American Democracy," *Yale Divinity News*, XXXVIII, no. 1, 3-4, November 1941.

"A Major Problem of Our Time," *The Union Signal*, January 24, 1942.

"Selective Service and the Ministry," *Yale Divinity News*, XXXVIII, no. 3, 1-2, March 1942.

"The War-time Service of the Yale University Divinity School," *Yale Divinity News*, XXXIX, no. 1, 1-3, November 1942.

"Religious Freedom," presidential address at meeting of the Federal Council of the Churches of Christ in America, at Cleveland, December 10, 1942. In the Biennial Report of the Federal Council of the Churches of Christ in America, 1942, pp. 29-35.

"Religious Freedom and Public Duty," *Yale Divinity News*, XL, no. 1, 1-3, November 1943.

"A Glimpse of the Divinity School: Excerpts from Report to the president of Yale University," *Yale Divinity News*, XLI, no. 1, 1-4, November 1942.

"Frank Chamberlin Porter," *Yale Divinity News*, XLII no. 3, 1-2, March 1946.

"The New New Testament," *International Journal of Religious Education*, XXII no. 7, 8-9, 31, March 1946.

"The Making of the Revised Standard Version of the New Testament," *Religion in Life*, XV no. 2, 163-173, Spring 1946.

"The Second Freedom," *Christian Herald*, 19, 85, March 1946. Reprinted in *Religious Digest*, 75-76, May 1946.

"Reformation Sunday, November 2," *Daily Devotions*, Fall 1947, Pilgrim Press.

"The American Tradition of Religious Freedom," *Social Action*, XIII, No. 9, 5-14 1947.

"The American Tradition of Religious Freedom," *The Lutheran Theological Seminary Bulletin*, Gettysburg, XXVIII, no. 3, 10-13, August 1948.

"The Rights of Religious Freedom," the concluding section of the presidential address at Cleveland, *Christian Education*, XXVI, no. 3, 145-147, March 1943. Also in *Current Religious Thought*, III, no. 1, January 1943. It appears also as Appendix IV in volume III of *Church and State in the United States*, by Anson Phelps Stokes, with the statement that "it is impossible to reproduce this important address in full, but the threefold analysis of the rights that may be claimed in the name of religious freedom is given below." New York: Harper & Brothers, 1950, pp. 897-899.

"Freedom of Religion and Education," *Christianity and Crisis*, X, 98-103, 1950.

"The Challenges Ahead for Church-related Colleges," *College and Church*, XV, no. 1, 12-20, Spring 1950.

"The Relevance of the Revised Standard Version of the Bible," *The Eighteenth Biennial Meeting of the American Association of Theological Schools*, Southern Baptist Theological Seminary, Louisville, Kentucky. Bulletin 20, 91-108, June 1952.

"The Revised Standard Version of the Bible: A Discussion of the Compelling Reasons which Made a New Revision of the Bible Necessary," *Pulpit Digest*, XXXII, no. 172, 11-16, August 1952.

"The Revised Standard Version of the Bible," *Lutheran Woman's Work*, October 1952.

"The Revised Standard Version of the Bible," *Catholic Biblical Quarterly*, XIV, 310-318, October 1952.

"In Appreciation of Fleming James," *Anglican Theological Review*, XXXIV, 200-202, October 1952.

"Connecticut, Yale, and the Christian Ministry," *Yale Divinity News*, XXXII, no. 1, November 1935.

"The Revised Standard Version of the Bible," *World Christian Education*, VIII, no. 1, 7-9, 17, January 1953.

"Revised Standard Version of the Bible Rich in New Text," *Chicago Tribune Magazine of Books*, pp. 2, 11, March 15, 1953.

"I Believe in the Bible," *The Church Woman*, April 1953.

"The Revised Standard Version," *The Christian Scholar*, XXXVI, no. 4, December 1953.

"The Crisis of Religion in Education," *Religious Education*, XLIX, 73-77, March-April 1954. Address at golden anniversary convention of the Religious Education Association, Pittsburgh, November 10, 1953. This address was printed earlier in *Vital Speeches of the Day*, 147-149, December 15, 1953.

"Scholarship, Education and the Bible," address at the 16th triennial convention of the Cum Laude Society. Reprinted from *The Proceedings*, New York, Division of Christian Education, National Council of Churches, CXLVII, 16, 1954.

"The Larger Hope," *Advance*, CXLVII, no. 8, April 20, 1955.

"The Living and Active Word," *Advance*, CXLVII, no. 14, 4-6, July 27, 1955.

"Christian Education and International Affairs," *The Ecumenical Review*, VIII, no. 4, 461-463, July 1956.

"The Fresh Appeal of the Bible," *World Christian Education*, XII, no. 3, 65, July 1957.

"And Now, The Apocrypha," *The New Christian Advocate*, I, no. 14, 28-30, November 1957.

"Why Use the RSV?" *Bible Teacher for Adults*, XVII, no. 1, 2-5, January 1962.

"Jesus' Prayers from the Cross," the Advocate Lenten Sermon Series, *The Methodist Christian Advocate*, Birmingham, Alabama, LXXXVI, no. 8, 1-2, 14, March 1, 1966.

"Our Educational Heritage through the Congregational Tradition," *The Church School Worker*, XVII, no. 1, 12-14, September 1966.

VI. Published Reports

Bulletin of Yale University: Reports made to the president by the deans and directors of the several schools and departments:

For the academic year 1928-1929: Divinity School, pp. 102-116
For the academic year 1929-1930: Divinity School, pp. 126-143
For the academic year 1930-1931: Divinity School, pp. 126-147
For the academic year 1931-1932: Divinity School, pp. 94-119
For the academic year 1932-1933: Divinity School, pp. 110-127
For the academic year 1933-1934: Divinity School, pp. 94-112

1

2

1. The young Luther Allan Weigle, left, with brother Daniel and sister Harriet (later Mrs. George Nicely), in Lancaster, Pa. about 1887.

2. Luther Allan Weigle as a Carleton College tennis coach, with his winning team.

3. Dr. and Mrs. Weigle with their children: back row, left to right: Richard D., Margaret (now Mrs. William F. Quillian), Luther Allan Jr.; front center: Ruth (now Mrs. Arthur C. Guyton). At the family cottage, Lake Sunapee, New Hampshire, about 1927.

4. Dr. and Mrs. Weigle on shipboard en route to the Rio de Janeiro convention of the World Sunday School Association, 1932.

5. Dr. Weigle confers with a student in the office of the Dean, Yale Divinity School.

4

5

7

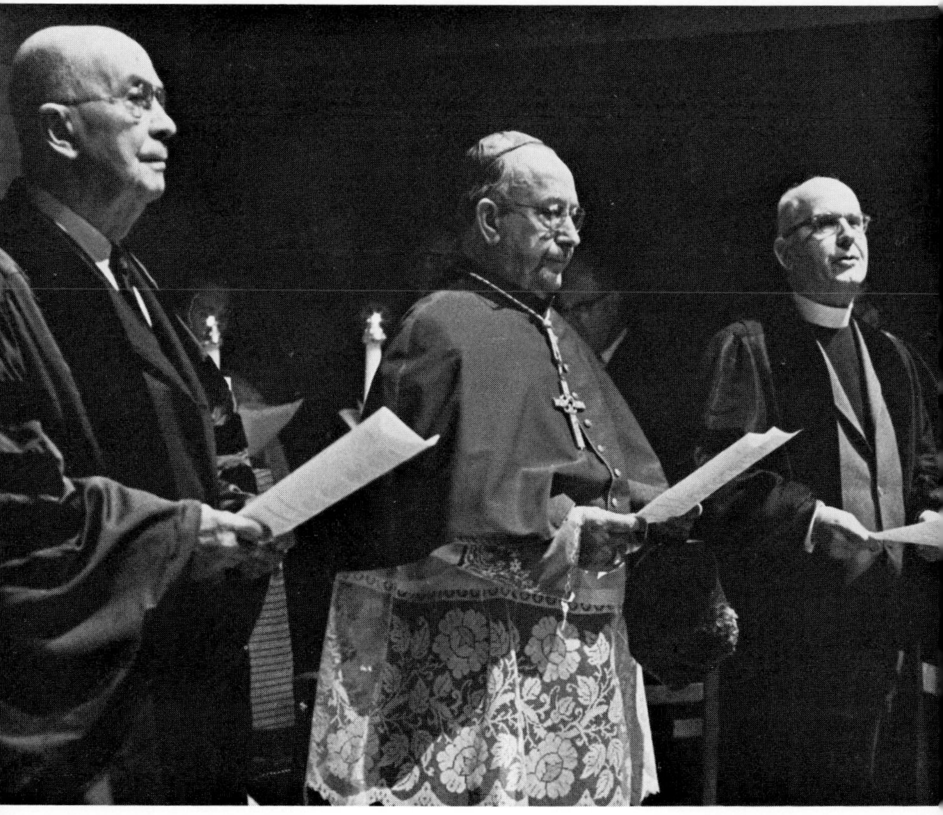

6. Dr. Weigle, right, presents the one-millionth copy of the Revised Standard Version of the Bible to Dr. Martin Niemoeller, famed pastor of the German resistance.

7. As Dr. Weigle is made a Knight of the Order of St. Gregory the Great, by action of Pope Paul VI, Archbishop Henry O'Brien of Hartford and Dr. Gerald E. Knoff of the National Council of Churches participate.

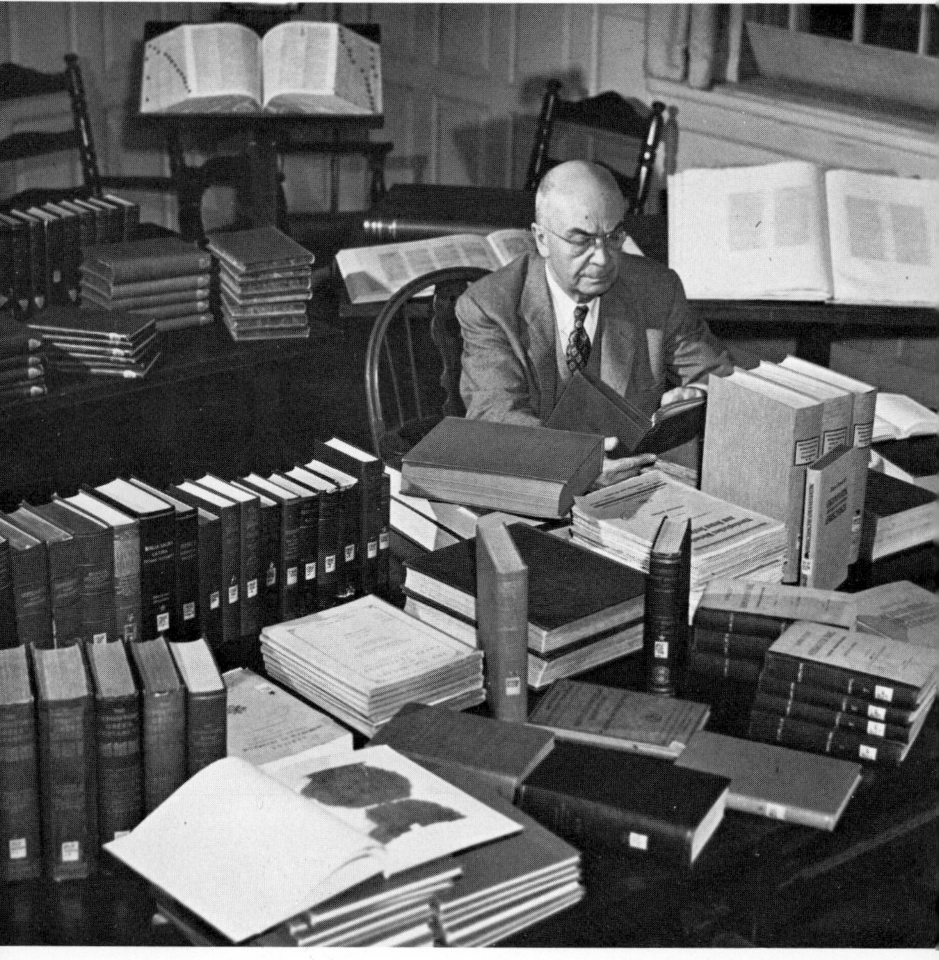

8. Hours beyond count were invested in detailed and scholarly study in preparation for the printing of the Revised Standard Version of the Bible.

9. Dr. Weigle poses on his 90th birthday with his four children.

10. Some members of the Planning Committee for the National Council of the Churches of Christ in the U.S.A., shown at a 1949 meeting with Dr. Weigle, front row, second from left.

9

10

11

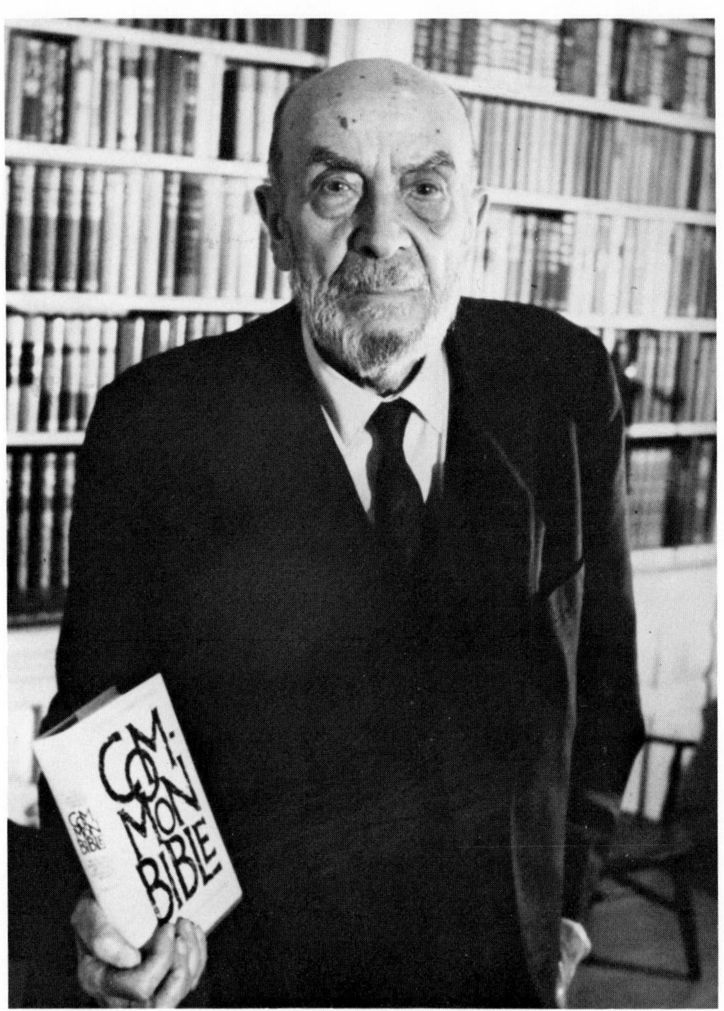

11. In a fitting climax to a great career, Dr. Weigle displays a copy of the Revised Standard Version Common Bible, hailed as "the Bible for all Christians."

PHOTO CREDITS

In order of appearance

1. The Fulton Studio, Lancaster, Pa.
2. C.J. Mehlin, Northfield, Minn.
3. Family collection
4. Ella Barnett, New York, N.Y.
5. Family collection

6 & 7. National Council of Churches

8. Yale University News Bureau – Alburtus
9. Evans Photographers, Hamden, Conn.
10. Religious News Service
11. Gene Gorlick, The New Haven Register